LIFE AT
FIRST SIGHT

For Matt and Kari—
Enjoy the journey ☺
May your spirits be
happy, and your days
and hours filled with
much joy.

Warmest good wishes,
Phyllis

LIFE AT FIRST SIGHT

*Finding
the Divine
in the
Details*

Phyllis Edgerly Ring

Bahá'í
PUBLISHING
Wilmette, Illinois

Bahá'í Publishing
415 Linden Avenue, Wilmette, Illinois 60091-2844
Copyright © 2009 by the National Spiritual Assembly of the
Bahá'ís of the United States
All rights reserved. Published 2009
Printed in the United States of America on acid-free paper ∞

12   11   10   09   4   3   2   1

Library of Congress Cataloging-in-Publication Data
Ring, Phyllis Edgerly.
  Life at first sight : finding the divine in the details / Phyllis Edgerly Ring.
      p. cm.
  Includes bibliographical references.
  ISBN-13: 978-1-931847-67-4 (pbk. : alk. paper)
  ISBN-10: 1-931847-67-3 (pbk. : alk. paper) 1. Religious life—Bahai Faith. I.
Title.

BP380.R56 2009
297.9'344—dc22
                                                    2008055037

Cover design by Robert A. Reddy
Book design by Suni D. Hannan

For Mum, Dad, and Tracey

CONTENTS

ACKNOWLEDGMENTS

How does one recognize all who help any sort of endeavor come together? The attempt could become a small book in itself.

I will first thank Lauren Chuslo Shur, whose encouraging question, "Why don't you write a column?" those many years ago was just the invitation I'd shyly been waiting for. Your support over the years has been invaluable company, and it's a double bonus that you've become such a good friend, too.

We met through an angel we know named Audrey Stomierosky, who shepherded many writers' words to higher ground. You had to leave us much too soon, Audrey, but I'm forever grateful for your mentoring and big-sister company, and I can feel your help still. Other valued helpers like Audrey who now assist from beyond the limits of this earthly life, and for whom I am eternally thankful, include Erik Blumenthal, Anthony de Mello, Daniel Jordan, Marian Lippitt, Ann Schoonmaker, Leonard Smith, and Charlotte Wood.

Few writers make it down the path to publication without cheerleaders and spiritual family like Kathy Gilman, the Grover Family, Jane Harper, Diane Kirkup, Carolyn Stoddard, and Ronnie Tomanio, and I thank you all.

Dru Cederquist and Rabi Musah each showed up in this writer's life when it required the spiritual kinship of wise and reflective communicators—and life brought me two of you at once, how about that? And for more than twenty-five years, the International Women's Writing Guild has provided me with that kind of companionship, too. My special thanks to its founder, Hannelore Hahn, and the hundreds of women who bring so much to the Guild's annual Skidmore conference each June.

My husband, Jon, didn't know that he was marrying a writer—neither did I, at the time. But how gracefully, and kindly, he has lived with and encouraged one these many years. And he has been my closest companion as I look for "life at first sight," wherever it may be found. Each of our children has also been generous in their support, especially since their lives were so often grist for my little mill. It touched me, Vanessa, when you'd tell me while you were away in China that the columns felt like "visits," and also a chance to get to know me better. And Tobey, I really appreciate that you'd ask about my progress with book projects the way a good friend would.

And Martina Amrita Fischer Dalecki—your spiritual companionship, exquisite literary perception, and the radiance of your love have so often been what has helped this writer imagine writing at all. Thank you, and all your dear extended family, for such a generous welcome back to the home my soul loves best in all the world.

Phyllis Edgerly Ring
January 19, 2009

INTRODUCTION

Around the time I first encountered the faith whose teachings have enriched my life for more than thirty years, a letter was sent by its international governing body, the Universal House of Justice, to those who had asked what the best response was to the suffering we encounter on an ever-increasing scale in our world. A portion of that letter summarized what, for me, has always felt like the meaning of our existence in this earthly life:

> It is not merely material well-being that people need. What they desperately need is to know how to live their lives—they need to know who they are, to what purpose they exist, and how they should act towards one another; and, once they know the answers to these questions they need to be helped to gradually apply these answers to everyday behavior. It is to the solution of this basic problem of mankind that the greater part of all our energy and resources should be directed.
>
> —The Universal House of Justice, letter dated 19 November 1974 to the National Spiritual Assembly of the Bahá'ís of Italy [1]

For idealistic materialists, the letter went on to explain, material good is often the only "real" good. However, from a more overall kind of vision, one that proceeds from our very soul, "the material world is merely a reflection of spiritual conditions and until the spiritual conditions can be changed there can be no lasting change for the better in material affairs."[2]

THREE ASPECTS OF OURSELVES, THREE KINDS OF "SEEING"

'Abdu'l-Bahá, the eldest son and appointed leader of the Bahá'í Faith after the passing of Bahá'u'lláh, its Prophet-Founder, modeled the practice of addressing the spiritual conditions that lie at the root of our most difficult problems. He set an example that repeatedly reinforced the reality that all true happiness comes from the spiritual aspect of life. He also illuminated the mystery of our creation and true purpose by describing three realities that comprise us: "an outward or physical reality . . . a second or higher reality which is the intellectual reality . . . a third reality . . . that is the spiritual reality."[3] Each of these aspects of ourselves seems to bring with it a particular level of perception.

The eyes of our bodies, our outer, physical aspect, deal with the world of matter. They are primarily concerned with survival. Though we are no longer prey for some other species, getting around safely and maintaining our life still requires paying some attention to the things of this world.

Beyond survival and the perpetuation of our species, however, material vision and preoccupation with the material world aren't intended to take up too much of our time and attention. Yet they do, and the result seems to be unending confusion and pain. Might this simply be because we're using this kind of vision beyond the scope of its real purpose and power?

Our intellectual aspect finds its vision in the eyes of our mind, our acquired knowledge and learning. This second type of vision has an advantage over the eyes of the body, as it is able to think about matters beyond the present, whereas our physical reality's sight is confined only to the present moment and getting through it— good for immediate, physical safety, but not so helpful for enduring relationships or building a future.

It is the vision of our mind that contributes to our ability to learn from our experience, and eventually shapes our individual worldview— the ideas we form about ourselves and what is most important to us. This can help increase our understanding, or it can dig us deeper into the kinds of misdirected and misinformed thinking that can tyrannize our life. 'Abdu'l-Bahá once described these as "fevers in the world of the mind," which can grow into "fires of war and hate, of resentment and malice among the nations," and ultimately destroy "the tranquillity of the whole world."[4]

It is the eyes of our heart, our spiritual nature, that have the greatest capacity and are able to offer the best view in our ongoing search for truth. From their vantage point, like an eagle soaring, we can see the wholeness of most anything. We can perceive what truly matters. Our experiences connected to the heart seem to unfailingly boost our sense of joy and happiness.

This vision, which is detached from the world and our own thoughts, also gradually dispels the shadows of any painful sense of separation or isolation that we might feel. The gentle light of witnessing reality with this highest kind of vision, through the eyes of our heart, gradually exposes our misinformed perceptions for the illusions they truly are, as the unity of everything in creation becomes undeniably apparent to us. Those who have had near-death experiences often describe a transition into this type of heightened and clear perception. But thankfully we don't all need to have near-death experiences to reach this state of being. Guidance found in most of the world's religious scriptures suggests that we can access this kind of vision by an act of choice or will through such tools as prayer, meditation, and reflection.

When we do access this spiritual sight, the light that gleams through to illumine our inner dark corners is evidence of the presence of the attributes of a Creator Who has fashioned us out of love. The liberating light of these divine attributes, and the love they bring with them, can glimmer in all sorts of places and circumstances. We might perceive them within a minute pebble, in the leaves of a tree, in the actions of our animal companions, and, in particular, within each other.

In fact, the illuminating light of these attributes of God often becomes real to us through our interactions with others. Every day of our lives we have the opportunity to perceive and witness these realities reflected in each other, as well as in the world around us. Opportunities present themselves in every moment, and within each one we can catch sight of glimpses of paradise, of the "Kingdom" that Christ talked about so long ago to his small band of beleaguered but steadfast Apostles.

EFFORT IS NEEDED

While the light of these spiritual realities shines without ceasing, much like the rays of the physical sun, our ability to detect and receive its warmth calls for a certain kind of willingness and effort on our part. It is not a given that we will simply see and feel them. The Creator's design seems to require that our perceiving them be a matter of conscious intent, of deliberately choosing to use the highest form of vision we possess.

Initially, as children, we often see these spiritual realities innately, seemingly as a matter of course. But whether we remember doing so or not, we all seem to eventually reach a crossroads where we need to personally decide whether or not we will continue to do so. In order to do this, we need to choose to turn our attention away from the two lower kinds of vision in favor of what can be revealed by our higher vision. In other words, to periodically turn away from the material world and quiet our thoughts so that something more may become apparent to us.

"Close one eye and open the other," Bahá'u'lláh counsels. "Close one to the world and all that is therein, and open the other to the hallowed beauty of the Beloved."[5]

Just how can we see that sacred beauty? Many call the kind of vision and perception that can see beyond the limits of time and space, the undeniable boundaries of this physical world, "second sight." But ever since I discovered the value of seeking this kind of timeless vision, I've been more inclined to call it "first sight."

I count myself very lucky that early on in my life I was shown the importance of choosing to employ this sight by a deeply wise octogenarian who had learned a great deal about the power of love. As Robert Frost might say, I was encouraged toward the road "less traveled by, and that has made all the difference."

Whenever I am willing to forgo dwelling on what the eyes of my body and mind insist they are seeing, and instead invite in that third kind of vision, two things unfailingly happen: those lovely attributes of God, and the love with which God fashioned creation, show themselves, often like little gemstones hidden in surprising places. And I feel an instant, enveloping, and reassuring sense of peace. Through the years, I've come to call these experiences "life at first sight."

Like love at first sight, using our spiritual vision involves an immediate "recognition" and irresistible attraction, a sense of something mysteriously familiar, and a feeling of reunion. Even love itself, it seems, is actually an invitation to the recognition of a deeper life that has no end or separation, the part of our lives that is the true and enduring source of all happiness.

EACH MOMENT MADE NEW

The recognition of the reality of this spiritual world, that "aha" moment we experience each time we feel it, is present every time we choose to see with our spiritual vision. Each experience feels "new" yet also brings with it a sense of timelessness. It's the eternal beauty inherent in every moment; the feeling of seeing the end in the beginning; the discovered treasure that feels as though it has always been there, and which, without fail, brings peace and joy even in the midst of fire and trials. It is that feeling of coming into contact with what is of God.

And how do we know, feel, and recognize what is of God? By coming into contact with the attributes of God—such divine qualities as kindness, courtesy, generosity, and courage. It is through our encounters with and recognition of these attributes that our own deepest power and potential seem to be called forth and our most all-encompassing sight is reinforced.

As with love at first sight, our attraction to this greater life also revolves around our recognition of certain qualities and attributes that are both inviting and familiar to us. Cultivating the ability and the desire to perceive these in the everyday, especially at first glance, may be one of the most life-sustaining and liberating things we'll ever do, the foundation of a life that consciously chooses happiness.

Living this way, by choosing to focus on the spiritual side of life, is a choice and a practice that stands in marked contrast to what the world has taught most of us. It affirms that we each have access to all that we truly need, that there is plenty for all of us, and that the perfection of divine design actually facilitates our being able to enhance this experience by sharing it together.

Each of the three aspects of ourselves has a specific power and purpose, and we are presented with choices in every moment about how to use them. The decisions we make based on these choices are enhanced by understanding the three different kinds of vision involved.

We can view what we encounter as matter, as what matters to us, or what truly matters. We can use the eyes of our body to ensure our survival, or to become lost in the sea of materialism that surrounds us. We can use the eyes of our mind to learn and gain new understanding, or to grope around in illusion and confusion, blindly imitating the past and remaining shrouded in numberless veils. We can use the eyes of our heart to transcend limitations by perceiving everything from that luminous reality of which we, too, are a part; or we can choose to ignore the eyes of our heart and use only the first two visions, never seeing all that we are capable of perceiving. We acquire a more complete picture of human reality—body, mind, and soul—I have found, by gradually learning to use all three kinds of seeing to the best of our abilities and discovering how they are designed to work together.

When I first began writing columns, my intent (and my editor's assignment) was to be a sort of commentator-companion for parents and other adults as they kept watch for those spiritual virtues and attributes treasured within children. I knew from my own experience just how precious and important those are, and how brightly they can shine. But I also knew how easily they can be overlooked, and even trampled underfoot, if one is not careful. One thing that I'd also discovered about these moments was that without a conscious effort to use the eyes of my heart, I would surely miss them.

Over the years, my search for and reflection on what mirrored these realities in life around me was bound to widen and grow, of course. Little by little, the columns and essays embodied my ongoing efforts (and struggle) to "close one eye and open the other," and with that other kind of vision, to try and perceive the abundant evidence with which the spiritual side of life surrounds us every day. When United Press International invited me to serve as a columnist for its Religion and Spirituality Forum, I received a weekly opportunity—and challenge—to go looking for that light.

Marian Lippitt, my dear spiritual godmother who encouraged me to use my "first sight" so many years ago, remains my most enduringly memorable example of the sheer happiness and delight that this approach to life brings. I often watched her mere presence transform a room, as at least one of these essays describes. Through the years, I've also encountered many other generous-spirited souls who show an unhesitating willingness to open and use those inner eyes and to share the joy that doing so brings.

Marian used to remind me of something that Jesus told His followers: "The Spirit of God is working in your midst."[6] Her life served as a beautiful reminder that it is through the spirit of faith that we find the vision that enables us to see the enduring truth of this reality with our own, most far-seeing eyes.

CHAPTER 1

A MORE POWERFUL THOUGHT OF LOVE

"When a thought of war comes, oppose it by a stronger thought of peace. A thought of hatred must be destroyed by a more powerful thought of love."

—'Abdu'l-Bahá, *Paris Talks*

The Hand That Gives Us Roses

*True generosity of spirit knows that giving and
receiving are two halves of one whole.*

At the school where our daughter teaches preschoolers, there's a poster whose words about kindness never fail to touch me. They're from an old Chinese proverb that says, "A bit of fragrance always clings to the hand that gives us roses."

Mother Teresa once described a similar truth when she said, "Kind words can be short and easy to speak, but their echoes are truly endless."[1]

I suspect that kind actions reverberate even more powerfully.

Recently a young relative of mine deepened my understanding about an operative principle in the practice of genuine kindness: having the confidence and faith that life itself is generous. The fragrance to which that Chinese proverb refers, that lingering sweetness in any gift or kindness, seems to be a reminder of this.

My nephew, a kindergartner, is mad for gumball machines, which means quarters have taken on a whole new significance for him. Now that these shiny silver coins represent a "ticket" to what's inside those dispensers of treats, he considers them a valuable commodity indeed.

Recently he was attending a sports event with his family and was given a quarter by a family friend. He slipped it into his pocket with the care we reserve for precious objects, wearing a big smile in anticipation of what it would later purchase for him.

Sometime later, during the game, the woman sitting behind him was munching from a bag of potato chips. This little boy turned to her and asked politely, "May I please have some chips, too?"

His family could have been embarrassed by this, of course. But the woman chose to validate how very politely he'd asked by happily sharing her snack with him. He's been taught quite a bit in his family about sharing and figured it was OK to ask about the chips.

Once the game was over, he and his family left the stadium and were soon walking along the sidewalk outside. When they passed a homeless person sitting on the sidewalk, my nephew's older sister noticed the cup on the ground beside the man and asked her dad, "Why does that man have the cup for money?"

Her father told her that it was possible the man didn't have a place to live, or very much money.

"Then why doesn't he work so that he can have money?" she wondered.

"Well, that would be a good way to get some money, but maybe he hasn't been able to find a job, or there's some reason why he can't work," her dad said.

After a pause, she said, "I wish he could have some money."

Tromping along beside her, her brother suddenly stopped and realized aloud, "*I* have some money!"

Without a second's hesitation, he bounded back toward the man on the sidewalk, no doubt causing his family members to turn and race to keep up with him on the busy street. With a smile at least as large as the one he'd had when he'd first pocketed that quarter, he fished the coin out and placed it carefully in the man's cup.

What struck me in his actions, aside from the unadulterated generosity of spirit, was the complete lack of hesitation he had in expressing a willingness either to receive or to share and give. He seemed to have an innate understanding of what a reciprocal pair these acts are, like two halves of one whole.

And of course, my nephew took kindness a step further when he so instantly embodied the golden rule enshrined in each of the world religions. In his worldview, life's a place that provides, and we're the actors in this reciprocal process. There's enough for everybody, and we all get to help it go around.

It's easy to imagine the recipient's response. I'm told that it was quite emotional. Along with money, that man also received spontaneous regard and friendliness, someone who looked him straight in the eyes and saw him. That's something in very short supply these days, particularly in lives like his. The exchange was something that no doubt will leave fragrance lingering on both sides for a long time to come.

There's No Such Thing as Small Change

*Change that moves away from blind imitation of the past
is nearly always an act of real moral courage,
however small it may appear at first.*

I was reminded recently of what a myth it is that people can't change, that generations of behaving a certain way only leads to more of the same.

Friends of ours have made enormous efforts as a couple, and a family, to help their neighborhood be a better place for kids. Once a thriving, middle-class community to which the husband's grandparents immigrated, it has, in recent decades, fallen into sad decay with their city's economic depression. Little by little, the couple's home—the house his grandparents bought long ago—became a safe haven for the neighborhood's kids, many of whom did not have much of a home life. Often their parents just didn't know how to get up after taking too many hits when they were already down.

As our friends and their own three children watched their home evolve into a de facto Boys and Girls Club, they decided to be intentional about it. They bought the house next door (an affordable prospect in a neighborhood where few choose to live) and invested in putting a pool in their backyard. Over the next decade of summers a lot of kids gathered around that pool. The warm welcome children from the neighborhood received there included rules, giving them a chance to develop self-discipline that most would find nowhere else.

The organized fun that those kids experienced revolved around the couple's efforts to offer them the biggest possible service—a chance to develop what Dr. Martin Luther King Jr. once called "the content of their character"—and to understand that this is the real purpose of life. Helping kids do this meant devoting their home to these activities every summer and offering scaled-down versions after school and during school vacations. It also meant being available at all hours and gradually assisting many of the children's parents, who came to trust them like family.

None of it was ever easy, and the sacrifices were huge. But our friends say they can't imagine any other life, and that their own marriage and family life benefited because of it. Many of the dozens of kids who passed through their house, and a number of their parents, have found possibilities in life they might never have known existed or thought possible.

I thought I knew this couple's story until, while I was visiting with them, the husband nodded toward a city bus stop as we drove past and said, "That's where it all began."

Over dinner, the two of them continued the story that began with their courtship and decision to marry shortly after high school. He described how, as they were standing at that bus stop one day, starry-eyed with love and making big plans for their future together, he'd said something offhandedly. A car of men with faces as dark as most of their neighbors today had driven by, and without even thinking, he'd uttered a racial slur. It was something he'd heard fairly frequently in his family, among his peers, and at that house his grandparents had lived in.

"I'll never forget the look on her face," he told me as he eyed his wife beside him. "That look in her eyes, it was a combination of disbelief and anger, disappointment and sadness." That look, he said, had made the biggest impact on him of all, unleashing changes he never could have predicted.

His wife explained that she'd grown up with her family's foster son, whom she truly loved like a brother, and who was black. The circle of her family's friends also included many African Americans. Hearing her future husband say something like this seemed unthinkable and unacceptable. As she turned to him with that sad and disillusioned look that day, she told him, "I don't think I can be with you."

At the time, her husband noted, any remorse on his part was motivated strictly by the desire not to lose her. "But I also didn't want to lose the love and trust and respect she had had for me that I saw leave her eyes when I'd said that," he explained. "And I knew that I wanted the mother of my children to be someone who had the strength of conviction that she had. It was brave to take a stand like that, because she really loved me, and what I said must have been a big disappointment to her."

Like the efforts they later made to help their neighborhood's children, nothing came easily or overnight. But he did have a kind of epiphany that day, he said. "I realized that I had more choice about what I could do, think, and believe than I had understood. A lot of my actions and beliefs came out of the way my family and those who I'd grown up with saw things, and it was my responsibility to recognize how I'd been influenced by that, and to decide what I wanted to believe and how I wanted to behave for myself."

Standing at the bus stop that day, he couldn't have imagined where such a willingness to change would lead him. Not only did that house his grandparents bought long ago eventually become an interracial community center, but his own circle of friends and family, an ever-widening one whose members he treasures, looks much different than it might have had he chosen a different path. That circle includes a kind young black man who became his son-in-law, and his daughter and son-in-law's three lively little granddaughters whom he and his wife love so much.

The kind of change that moves away from blind imitation of the past is nearly always an act of real moral courage, however small it may appear at first. The smallest action or decision to change based on principles or new understanding can often be overlooked by others, seemingly invisible at the time. But as my friends—and their many friends—can testify, it initiates a quietly powerful momentum that, like the lever of Archimedes, can sometimes move the world.

Every True Gift Has Eternity in It

Carol's example consistently modeled what it means to choose the more powerful and effective option of love.

My friend, Carol, gave me a wonderful surprise at about the last place I'd ever have expected it—her funeral.

She had a knack for surprising me, usually by helping me see life a little differently. Through knowing her, I came to understand just how much I have to be thankful for—or even simply how much I *have,* since her own life was mostly one of learning how to do without.

She had this remarkably stylish way of taking care of those few things she did have, treating those possessions with an elegant care, as though they were some sort of sacred trust. This made everything she owned (and was typically more than willing to share) seem far more special.

I remember thinking to myself at one point that if you gave Carol a gift, it was something she was really, demonstrably, going to appreciate and find a way to use meaningfully. There was spirituality in the way she related to the goods she received that quietly reminded me to be more mindful. Impoverished by this culture's standards, she embodied Bahá'u'lláh's teachings about how to function as a spiritual being in a material world: "Be generous in prosperity, and thankful in adversity. . . . Be a treasure to the poor, an admonisher to the rich, an answerer of the cry of the needy, a preserver of the sanctity of thy pledge. . . . Be a home for the stranger, a balm to the suffering . . ."[2]

Carol's example consistently reminded me that we should always choose the more powerful and effective option of love.

I heard about her cancer sometime during the summer. It seemed that Carol received the devastating news about her illness the very same day her employer told her she would soon be out of a job. I experienced that awful, helpless feeling you get when someone so good suddenly seems so unfairly punished.

Things happened fast for Carol after that. Although she endured the agony of treatment, her prognosis only got bleaker. By early September, she'd been given three months to live. Her goal was to make it through all three of them, which, God willing, would be just enough time to see her first grandchild born to the daughter who was her lifelong joy.

I made a trip to see her that week, together with two other friends. When we arrived at her small apartment and saw her, it was obvious that she wasn't going to make her goal. A home-health nurse admitted her to the hospital that same afternoon, and she died a few days later.

I had brought her a small CD player the day we visited her. She was feeling so terrible that even reading and watching TV were impossible, but she could still enjoy listening to music. However, her own CD player had broken.

It was enormously important to me to find her a new one. There was so much I couldn't bring her, so much I couldn't do for her. This, at least, seemed like one small thing I could offer. Knowing how weak she was, I searched for a little machine that was lightweight and, hopefully, something she'd be able to move herself.

The day I saw her, despite the fact that she was essentially drifting between worlds, she, as always, received my gift graciously. But my heart was deeply saddened by two things that were clear from the moment we watched the ambulance take her away: Carol was never going to use that CD player, and she wasn't going to live to see her grandchild born.

A little more than a week later, I sat in a small Victorian church whose beautiful stained glass windows flooded its golden-oak pews with rosy light. As we waited for the funeral service to begin, I was thinking about Carol, and her life, and all of the things that would never be, when I noticed that among the vases of cut flowers and the pretty candles that had been set out on a small table up front, there was something familiar.

Its display window glowed with the most amazing jewel shades of amethyst, emerald, and sapphire, shifting like the colors of a mood ring as it filled the church not with organ music or hymns, but the soothing voice of Bobby Darin, Carol's all-time favorite. I smiled because I'd never even noticed this quirky colors feature on that little CD player when I bought it, yet this is exactly the kind of thing Carol herself would have chosen and liked. I felt so glad to know that my gift had found a sense of purpose somewhere in her life after all.

But it wasn't until I had a conversation with her daughter afterward that I learned how wonderfully true this was.

"Oh," she told me, "I was so happy when I found that CD player in her things. I'm going to put it in the nursery and then Mom and the baby and I will all be able to listen together."

As I hugged her, Carol was as present with us in that moment as I know she will be in that nursery. It seems that in the fast-forward months when she battled cancer, lost her job, and struggled financially, Carol, who would have dearly loved to buy gifts for her grandchild, never had the chance (or the means) to do so.

"But then, here was this gift she was able to give to me and the baby after all," her daughter remarked.

At their most meaningful, our efforts at gift-giving invite a bigger process, one that involves the giving and receiving of love into our lives and into the lives of the people we wish to honor. Thank you, Carol, for helping me to understand this in a way I will never forget.

A Timely Dose of the Best Medicine

While we may have to dig deep some days to find the humor in the human experience, the effort itself can be a kind of healing balm.

This year, my mother gets a "real" birthday. Because she was a leap year baby, she often had to make do with birthday wishes either a day early or a day late. But this year, *she* seems to be the one sending out the messages, and with timely style, too.

I recently found two dreamy-looking photos of her taken not long before she died, presumably by my father, who was always insistent about taking photographs. I did a double take on first glance, because in those photos, she really does seem to be peering back at you from the mist of some world beyond this one.

I discovered these photos in a box of my parents' belongings, and close to these I found four small pages of stationery with my mother's distinctive handwriting filling up all eight sides. Just a few lines in, and I knew what this forgotten missive was—a collection of snapshot-style vignettes as she recalled them from the years when my parents and my then preschool-aged sister lived in postwar France and Germany.

"I decided then that you'd probably grow up to be a tactful, diplomatic person," she said of my sister, describing the time when, on her very first airplane flight (from London to Bordeaux, France), she, then four, made polite conversation with the two travelers seated face-to-face across from her and my mother. My mother describes them as "dressed in the full regalia of those who live in Arab countries."

If my mother only knew just how prophetic this statement would turn out to be. My sister grew up to work in Washington for three congressmen and a U.S. senator and had many, many opportunities to practice both tact and diplomacy.

Next in her recollections came a series of events from "Tu et You," my parents' nickname for the exceptionally rustic farmhouse where they were billeted when my father was first serving in France. "The toilet was directly off—almost still within—the kitchen," my mother writes. "The septic tank, it turns out, was directly under the toilet," as she had occasion to discover when said toilet malfunctioned and the horse-drawn "Vidange Rapide" ("quick drain") cart came to the rescue. The operator, she records, consumed a sandwich during the repair, all while periodically jiggling the leaky hose he was wielding. His verdict: "Too much tissue." Apparently none was the preferred quantity.

Each weekday, from the time my sister turned five, two military police would arrive at the house shortly before dawn to escort her to school via military staff car, a ride that took an hour each way. I cannot imagine what this meant for my mother's peace of mind each day, and it explains a lot about why my sister is probably one of the most flexible, unflappable travelers I know.

On some of those school days, my mother and a very pregnant neighbor, also a military spouse, would head off to the nearby market town to do laundry. My mother handled the French-speaking, at which she was quite adept, and the neighbor provided the transportation. My mother was tasked with planning their route, which she did very carefully, as the neighbor's Studebaker had no reverse gear.

On one of those days, Henri the gardener decided to "repair" the coal stove and inadvertently dislodged the stove pipe, which collapsed and blanketed everything in sight, including Henri, in soot. My mother noted that he did not stick around to help clean it up.

On New Year's Eve at the luxurious Grand Hotel in Bordeaux, the elegant doors to the rooms for "hommes" (men) and "femmes" (women) opened into the same restroom. "And the very fancy chicken entrée still had most of its insides," my mother noted. As she did on most occasions, she would come home afterward and sit on my sister's bed and share a host of details about the evening, including descriptions of the most fashionably dressed women.

Then it was on to Frankfurt for the first of several tours my family would spend in Germany, one of which would eventually include me. Many military families had a maid, in part because so many postwar Germans needed the work. Ria, the first, asserted her influence with furniture: "Every weekend, your father would rearrange the gigantic German furniture, including the piano, and every Monday, Ria would put it all back. 'Nein, nein—dies ist besser,' she would always say."

Harriette favored "snail and Crisco sandwiches," and Olga, who had been a Russian prisoner of war (and suffered who knows what atrocities) hadn't seen a flush toilet before and thought it a fine device for cleaning vegetables, my mother was horrified to discover one day.

My discovery of this little collection of memories was perfectly timed for sending on to my sister, as she'd just passed triumphantly through cancer-related surgery that had delivered even better news than she'd let herself expect. I knew how very much she missed our mother at times like these—and my mother, true to form, came through.

Who knows where she'd tucked these little pages after she'd written them, probably not long before she died. She knew her days were numbered, and she was very systematic about organizing her things. Yet somehow this letter, written specifically with my sister in mind, didn't find its way into the mail until a time when it would bring her particular comfort.

Now, my father, who tended to be the family storyteller, used to regale us with stories like these for years, and no matter how many times we heard them, they would send tears of mirth rolling down our cheeks.

My mother's dry summaries, with their wry British wit, certainly did too. Yet there is something that also speaks volumes between their terse lines. My father, more often than not, came home to hear about these experiences, while my mother, with a battlefront whose local dialect kept changing, actually lived them.

Humor was obviously a very big part of how she managed that. And while some days she may have had to dig deep to find that humor, the effort itself is still a kind of healing balm, even all these years later.

I was reminded of how Bahá'u'lláh's son 'Abdu'l-Bahá would often gather together those followers who'd been imprisoned with his father because of their belief in the Bahá'í Faith and have them recount the most ludicrous events of the day they could think of until everyone had a good laugh. There were undoubtedly times when they, too, had to really search to find some laughable part of those grueling days. But because they were willing to try, they always could.

21

CHAPTER 2

LODESTONE OF THE HEARTS

"A kindly tongue is the lodestone of the hearts of men.
It is the bread of the spirit, it clotheth the words with meaning,
it is the fountain of the light of wisdom and understanding."

— Bahá'u'lláh, *Epistle to the Son of the Wolf*

A Language That Needs No Translation

A smile, a kind look, an encouraging gesture are all
something we can recognize wherever we go,
whatever our mother tongue.

Few things are as eye-opening as learning how difficult it can be to communicate when you are in a country that does not use your own language, a fact I reencountered recently when I spent six weeks in my childhood home.

I first went to Germany at the age of four, where I developed a curious mix of German and English that I'd use with anyone willing to listen. My husband and I have made several return visits to this mutual home of our childhoods. Like me, he lived in Germany as a child with his military family, just a few miles from where my own family was stationed. Unlike me, he retained his German, along with a polished accent that convinces native speakers that he must be fluent.

In our first visits there I wanted to trot out whatever remnants of German I'd squirreled away, but felt too shy as I watched my husband conversing fluidly. I didn't possess that same "correct" accent, and the stage fright of trying to speak another language on the spot only seemed to accentuate that fact. I suddenly understood why our daughter, whose overseas living experience eventually gave her fluency in Mandarin, was initially unwilling to practice speaking it in front of anyone she actually knew.

However, I was determined to grasp this language in which I'd once been so immersed, at least enough to converse with some of the wonderful friends we've made in Germany without their having to drag out what little they could remember from their high-school English classes. I wanted to share the intimacy of communicating with people I care about in their own language. And, I admit, I wanted the secret pleasure of seeing in their faces the kind of surprise that illuminated the glazed-over eyes of Shanghai taxi drivers when our daughter addressed them politely in pitch-perfect Chinese.

So, true to my personal learning style, I took my efforts underground. (When I set a goal, I generally have the resolve to reach it, but see no reason to set myself up for public humiliation in the process.) I kept my study to myself as I bought a variety of German/ English dictionaries and phrasebooks and stocked my car with conversational CDs. After the first fifty miles or so, I could tell you all about train schedules for Erfurt and Ulm, how to book a double room, or find the breakfast room or bank.

I found German news sites on the Internet and read aloud from them, ordered German/English magazines and made myself read the German version first. As I gained vocabulary, I swapped my Bahá'í prayer book for one in German.

When it was time for me to actually practice speaking, the perfect partner arrived—the Miniature Schnauzer we inherited when my dad moved into assisted living. I wasn't ready for two-way exchanges yet anyway, and I knew she'd keep my confidence. Plus, as I told her, "This is the language of *your* ancestors, after all."

In early July, my husband and I flew to Frankfurt to begin a three-week vacation together, after which I stayed on for nearly as long with our German friends. As I read maps and road signs, I was secretly pleased at how readily I pronounced even the most multisyllabic names. I shopped easily without the need of an interpreter (usually my husband) and ordered meals without asking for the English menu.

And I was reminded again about how much knowing a language goes well beyond words. There are, of course, many nuances and unspoken elements that go with being fluent in a language, which, by default, means you've become fairly conversant with a culture, as well. For example, one difference I noticed between the United States and Germany is that German restaurants and cafés are usually much quieter places than those here at home, so much so that Americans can feel downright self-conscious in them, at first. Eventually you realize that people haven't stopped talking because you're there. They simply operate at more reserved decibels, something very helpful and considerate in a country with lots of small spaces. Conversely, complete strangers unfailingly greet you upon your arrival and departure in these same public spaces, and look surprised if you don't do the same—even though they may not say another word to you throughout your meal.

During my time in Germany, as I worked at learning how to understand those around me, both their language and their culture, I often wondered if there might be a common denominator for achieving some of that cultural fluency, even when you don't know the language. Among the wealth of guidance that Bahá'u'lláh has offered for uniting a very diverse world is the adoption by all nations of an international auxiliary language. Taught during childhood in addition to one's native tongue, this will help establish a world that is "as one land and one home"[1] for everyone. We see every day in international news why such a tool is essential if we want to move past the kinds of misunderstandings that consistently pose barriers to amicable association and agreement.

When I taught English to kindergartners in China, the curriculum I used also introduced another, more universal language that I believe human beings everywhere are preprogrammed to speak: the language of virtues. Living in a country where you can't speak the language, as I did, you gain new appreciation for spiritual characteristics as facilitators for communication and relationship building. A smile, a kind look, an encouraging gesture are all something we can recognize wherever we go, whatever our mother tongue.

Ironically, while I was in Germany, my fledgling attempts at actually speaking the language were significantly enhanced when I'd relax and look into the eyes of whomever I was trying to communicate with. Then the gems of human goodness we all seek became more visible, and it was amazing how much I understood intuitively. My unforgettable afternoon with Olga, the lovely woman from Kyrgyzstan who married our friend Ralf, was a poignant reminder of this. German is a second language for both of us, and while our conversation was necessarily limited, our tears and laughter demonstrated that we found an ability to communicate that went far beyond words.

In fact, since I couldn't fall back mindlessly on words during my six-week adventure, I found myself listening on a much deeper level. I was repeatedly surprised at how quickly I could connect with others when there was less focus on words, when I was unafraid of silence, and more willing to practice *presence*. This contact felt soul-to-soul, almost a euphoric kind of telepathy at times.

I don't know what the universal auxiliary language of which Bahá'u'lláh speaks will be, or whether I'll even live to see it at work in the world. But I do feel as though I've caught a glimpse of what surely must be one of its essential ingredients: the vocabulary of virtues that God has treasured inside each of us, that seems to find its best expression in actions and gestures of kindness, and that needs no translation at all.

Cultivating a Culture of Encouragement

Perhaps the very scarcity of encouragement in daily life is
what has so many feeling weary, fearful, and uninspired.

A friend once described how, when traveling on a bus in Africa, where many roads look like something Americans would reserve for all-terrain vehicles, he'd had an unexpected encounter with the power of encouragement.

Navigating such rutted routes is a formidable task. He noted that his fellow passengers would repeatedly, and with great enthusiasm, cry out a phrase that sounded to his ears like "ay-kushay." As he watched more carefully, he realized that this was a kind of cheer they made each time the driver successfully avoided a pothole.

His story brought to mind the friends I made when I lived in China. Seldom have I seen people work as hard or live with so little. In addition to showing a generally uncomplaining and positive attitude, they demonstrated something whose effectiveness finally makes sense to me. As they'd wave me on my way, they'd unfailingly call out, "Do your best," "Take your time," or "Enjoy yourself!"

It wasn't until I got back to the United States and no longer heard these things that I realized how much I'd appreciated such sources of encourage-ment. They had a lovely sound to my ears—and they were empowering.

To "encourage" each other, meaning literally "to give heart," is one of the most beautiful, godly gifts we can share. Perhaps the very scarcity of encouragement in daily life is what has so many feeling weary, fearful, and uninspired.

A good reason to cultivate encouragement is that its opposite, discouragement, tends to breed complaint and criticism like weeds. Falling prey to these feelings, which do nothing to draw us nearer to God, is all too easy, but surprisingly, practicing encouragement instead doesn't require much more effort.

As always, my best teachers about encouragement are those two young people who were supposed to have benefited from my parenting over the past couple of decades. I often think the main benefit they derived was from watching me repeatedly make mistakes that they could choose not to repeat. That's possibly what helped teach them the real value of encouragement, too, and they've picked up a few creative ideas about how to share it.

For years I'd wanted to plant a vegetable garden but had avoided doing so out of fear of failure. This probably stems from a discouraging remark someone once made about the hue of my thumb and the quality of my previous efforts. Whether or not our son is aware of this botanical neurosis of mine, he did a curious thing one spring weekend, announcing, "It's time to have a garden here this year."

I assumed that he, a plant lover with emerald-green growing capabilities, was going to implement and take charge of this idea, especially when, within hours, he'd borrowed equipment and proceeded to till up most of the backyard, leaving us with no choice but to plant one. Then he became increasingly unavailable. I was stunned, then anxious, as I (and our neighbors) continued to survey that sea of churned-up earth each day.

Finally, desperate, I asked my friend Judi if she could help me get started. She's someone who's seldom intimidated by anything, and her company was an immediate reassurance. We had a fine time that day as we shopped for plants and seeds and then planted them together. My anxieties seemed to melt away. She continued to offer me encouragement, as did my son whenever he noted and admired some new addition I'd made. Then one summer day, when something very discouraging had happened in my son's life, he threw himself into helping me create a beautiful perennial bed, and we both felt wonderful afterward.

As my growing plant kingdom daily taught me more about life and character traits (you can try to get rid of weeds by covering them up, but eventually you have to pull them out by their roots), it also showed me that encouragement tends to breed more of itself. Neighbors started stopping by to cheer me on, and I got to thank them later by giving away some of our harvest. And even more satisfying than that was that the time I spent digging and planting in my backyard included some of the hours I've felt closest to God.

One of the purposes of the teachings of the Bahá'í Faith is to help make visible the reality that God's creation is like a wondrous garden in which all races and cultures are intended to live as one family. Bahá'ís hope that our own experience of cultivating unity among all people, challenging as it inevitably is, will be a source of encouragement to all.

If love and encouragement can benefit one humble little garden, imagine their dynamic possibilities in each and every one of our relationships.

"Think we'll have a garden again this year?" my son asked with an encouraging twinkle in his eye when the following spring rolled around.

"How soon can you borrow the rototiller?" was my reply.

Be in No Hurry to Share Bad News

In a life of ups and downs, "bad" news can often be incomplete
or invalid. It might simply be a stage in the process of
change that may very well turn out for the good.

Toward the end of summer, I was savoring a more tranquil flavor and overall zest in my life that I'd attributed to the season itself. Then I realized that I'd watched virtually no television for three months. I'd seldom had the radio on, either.

For the last few years, I've been somewhat selective about what I watch and listen to anyhow. But my media-free season meant that a near-constant stream of anxiety-provoking "information" had suddenly been absent from my life. And, of course, the usefulness of that information has certainly been called into question for me.

Perhaps it was the trips I'd made to several different countries in recent years that underscored for me the disparity between events that occur in our world and the way in which they're packaged and reported to us here at home. As I witnessed increasing levels of either anxious or dispirited, or even downright dejected, responses in the face of unending "bad" news from media sources, I began to wonder: Are we exercising our capacity to reflect on the information presented to us? Are we asking good questions? Are we communicating honestly with each other in an effort to discover what the reality of circumstances and situations might be? Are we inquiring after the truth of a matter? Or are we simply receiving what we're being handed and reacting to it as though it's the ultimate end and truth?

I've been intrigued by a concept that encourages being eager to share good news but taking our time about sharing bad news. Might that be because good news often seems to empower people while bad news so often has the opposite effect?

I'm also beginning to think that in a world that's such a mixture of ups and downs, "bad" news is often incomplete or invalid. It's frequently simply a stage in the process of change that may very well turn out ultimately to be for the good. Emphasizing its awfulness, however, can paralyze a lot of wills along the way, and can encourage a culture of fear and hopelessness that keeps many from making the positive contributions that they otherwise may have been able or willing to make.

During my retreat from a relentless broadcast of ain't-it-awful, I also noticed how much of it leans toward something I haven't missed one bit—an insidious, even increasingly flagrant, gossipy tone that "popular" (says who?) culture seems duty bound to insert into everything. In fact, when folks around me begin to rev up on a bad-news or gossip track now, I find I'm ready to simply leave the gathering if it's not possible to change the subject to something that might take our thoughts to some place more useful.

In the Bahá'í Faith, backbiting is forbidden. *Forbidden* is a strong, unambiguous word that reminds me that this is an absolute. It is a law on par with stealing or murder, because it is also the source of much sorrow and destruction. Bahá'u'lláh urges that we "regard backbiting as a grievous error, and keep . . . aloof from its dominion, inasmuch as backbiting quencheth the light of the heart, and extinguisheth the life of the soul."[2]

Socrates has been credited with a dandy little mechanism for filtering out this sort of "fire extinguisher" from our lives. A story that's gone around the block far more than once still offers some timely wisdom about this.

It's said that the philosopher was approached one day by an acquaintance who couldn't wait to let him in on some information about a person they both knew. Before hearing him out, Socrates asked first that this information be submitted to a sort of triple-filter test. The first of those filters, he said, was truth. Was the acquaintance absolutely certain that what he was about to say about this other person was true?

It seems that the acquaintance had simply heard it from someone else, a common method of acquiring information, of course, but not a means by which he could confirm that it was true.

So, Socrates told him, since he didn't really know whether the information was true, it was time to apply the second filter, the filter of goodness. Was what the acquaintance was about to share about their friend something good?

A fair question, although most things that others rush to share in secret are seldom good, as was the case in this instance.

So, Socrates surmised, this man wanted to tell him something bad about another person, even though he wasn't certain that it was true. There was still one test remaining, the filter of usefulness. Is what the man wanted to tell him about his friend something that would be useful to the hearer? It's easy to guess the answer and to understand why Socrates politely passed on the opportunity.

If more of us do the same, the demand for sensationalized news will definitely go down. And maybe, with time, "popular" media will be something I'm likely to turn to again.

Every Sacred Trust Is on Loan

*Our human nature usually wants to take better care
of something that we know must be returned and
for which we'll be held accountable.*

Stories I recently heard from two women I know reinforced for me the importance of truly understanding the nature of spiritual stewardship. The most sacred trusts we're given as humans, even our own souls, it seems, are actually "on loan."

I recall how shocked I was to discover the fiercely protective, almost overwhelming maternal instincts that kick in after a child joins your family. Although some chalk this up to hormones, I've seen it activated in parents who've welcomed children through adoption, so I believe it must be a more complex matter.

And just as parents are often seized with this intense instinct that wants to hold on, they also have to find the inner ability to let go if those children they love are ever going to have a full life. As the well-known author and poet Khalil Gibran so sagely observed, "Your children are not your children. They are the sons and daughters of life's longing for itself. They come through you but not from you, and though they are with you yet they belong not to you."[3]

One friend found that Gibran's words took on new meaning after a trip to the children's room of her local library. When she arrived home with an armload of picture storybooks, they caused as much delighted fuss as those she'd previously ordered from a children's book club. But the difference with these books was that she and her kids were much more conscious that they were borrowed and would need to be responsibly cared for during the time they were with their family.

"I suddenly had a whole new view of just what parenthood truly implies," she said. "The care we show for what's been 'loaned' to us, the humility required to treat such relationships like a borrowed trust, means everything." When her children are eventually "returned," she'd like to think that they'll be "a bit well-worn with hugs" and also the obvious recipients of good listening and attention that they'll in turn be able to show to others. Although it isn't always the case, our human nature usually wants to take better care of something that we know must be returned and for which we'll be held accountable. This could be our children, or it could also be jobs entrusted to us, or even our own bodies.

Another friend, also a mother, came to understand this concept much earlier in her family's life than she ever expected to. Her first child was born at twenty-three weeks, and she watched him live in a neonatal nursery for two months before she had to say good-bye to him. Today, as the mother of an adopted child and another biological child who was also born prematurely, she sees those two months as a very significant lifetime, an extremely important "loan term."

While this baby was struggling to live, his mother was physically, emotionally, and spiritually at one of the lowest ebbs of her life. Watching him through the plastic incubator as he labored for each breath was one the most difficult times she had yet experienced. There were days when she wondered whether she would be able to bear this ordeal and get through it.

The baby's very circumstances precluded her from doing much of anything for him in terms of physical interaction or care, although she dutifully pumped her breast milk to feed him. She says that what she gave this small life, shared with her for such a short time, involved capacities she hadn't yet been able to find in herself, and I think that's a true metaphor for what the most significant part of any kind of loving is really all about. Because of her love for this tiny life, even though she knew she was going to lose him soon, she found a new way to receive and appreciate what each day brought, even though she couldn't be sure whether that day would be his last. She received it on its own terms, she says—and showed up at the hospital each day, even though there were days she didn't want to, simply to honor him and whatever part he had come to play in her life.

The resolution of the pain she inevitably felt during those months came when she realized just what Gibran is saying: that greater forces send our children—and our challenges—to us, and it's the way that we respond to these gifts with a willingness to learn and receive, whatever the circumstances, that is the greatest thing we can do.

She showed up at the hospital every day, sometimes several times a day, and let herself fall in love with someone she knew she wouldn't have in her life for very long, and accepted whatever short amount of time they could share together. She learned to let herself feel and honor every bit of the pain she was experiencing and, at the same time, to relish the joy and sweetness her little son had brought with him.

Although accepting the fact that we're designed to embrace both joy and pain can sometimes be a difficult lesson to learn, it's an important one for children to receive from their parents. We have a lot of anguish, struggle, and addiction today because we live in a culture that fears age, death, difficulty, and disability, and children usually don't see modeled for them the acceptance of both joy and pain as part of the course of life.

This concept of children being "borrowed" reaches outside the span of our families, too, as each of us shows up in others' lives like a gift on loan. Every interaction we have holds the potential to enhance the lives of others, to make the most of the "borrowed" time we're given.

All parents can benefit from the interactions others share with them that honor the sacred job of looking after our little charges that are sent out on "loan" to us. My friend with the stack of library books is a single mom as well as a doctor, and every bit of interest and involvement that others show toward her family feels like a precious gift. The mother of that little baby who died so soon was awfully lonely in those days when she was going back and forth to the hospital to visit him. Things as simple as mowing her lawn or driving her to the hospital, let alone actually stopping by just to be with her and listen, became more important than she ever could have imagined.

No matter what our beliefs, viewing all children and each other as belonging to something greater than any of us seems like a good place to lay the foundation for a world that might, finally, find its way to peace. Because after all, this planet is really only on loan to us, too.

CHAPTER 3

THE SWEETEST CONVERSATION

"There is nothing sweeter in the world of existence than prayer. Man must live in a state of prayer. The most blessed condition is the condition of prayer and supplication. Prayer is conversation with God. The greatest attainment or the sweetest state is none other than conversation with God. It creates spirituality, creates mindfulness and celestial feelings, begets new attractions to the Kingdom and engenders the susceptibilities of the higher intelligence."

—'Abdu'l-Bahá, *Star of the West*

Hope Blossoms with Prayer

*Prayer is a precious resource not because it makes problems go away,
but because it changes our experience and our perceptions within them.*

One summer day, I made a call to my sister that left me unable to get out of my chair afterward.

As I gazed out my office window at the lush blooms erupting in every direction, I thought, "This conversation and these surroundings can't be occurring in the same moment. I call to wish my sister a happy birthday in her favorite season, and she's telling me that she's just come home with a breast-cancer diagnosis."

There's such an incredible feeling of helplessness when we have to watch someone we love shoulder a burden that demands the deepest bravery while they are facing a challenge that reduces them to their most vulnerable. Everything about this development in my sister's life happened fast, from the discovery of the tumor to the surgery scheduled just a day later. I wanted so much to book a flight so I could be with her, to be able to feel like there was something I could do.

But instead I needed to turn my attention to the high-season pace of the Bahá'í conference center where I worked, where forty junior-high students were due to arrive in an hour and it was my job to get them settled in.

Then, shortly on the heels of my sister's call, came a call advising me that one of the cabin counselors for the kids' session wasn't going to be able to make it, and the only person available to take her place and serve as sleep-in chaperone for eleven preadolescent girls seemed to be me.

I experienced a wide range of feelings that afternoon. They included shock, disbelief, sadness, anger, and perhaps biggest of all, survivor's guilt, plus plenty of fearfulness. I also experienced a strange, hollow place inside where I seemed to feel nothing at all. Maybe that's what helped me get through those next hours until it was finally time to enforce curfew for those preteen girls.

When a coworker approached me excitedly that afternoon with news about an art exhibit she'd been invited to take part in, my response was one I'd need to make amends for later. I knew that her paintings were an important emotional release for her and often helped her find the heart to do the hard work required of us, especially during the summer months. But I wasn't a very supportive listener or friend that day. I was too immersed in the pain of my own troubles.

However, I did manage to do one thing I've felt grateful for ever since. I went back to her a few hours later to apologize, and when she heard about what was on my mind, she spontaneously offered what would prove a far-reaching response. She put her arms around me quietly for a few welcome moments, then promised to pray both for me and my sister. She even asked shyly whether I might like to say some prayers together. I was happy that she offered, because I hadn't been able to get to that myself quite yet.

After our prayers together I definitely felt better, or at least different, as I contemplated the night ahead, one in which I was sure I wouldn't get much sleep, and after which I'd still have to struggle through another ten-hour work day.

I had just been thinking about my sister when the phone rang and she was the caller. All of the arrangements were in place for her surgery the next day, she told me. Then she surprised me by saying, "I don't know what happened this afternoon, but I suddenly felt a wonderful shift that's made me feel such peace ever since, despite everything that's happening."

She went on to describe a decision she'd made to plant bougainvillea on the balcony of her town house as soon as her recovery was past. She'd seen the plant during her travels in the Caribbean and had always wanted to plant some but had been afraid the mid-Atlantic climate wouldn't support it.

"But I'm going to take the chance this year and see what happens. I'm going to fill the deck with it," she told me.

Within those words I heard her confidence, even faith, as she went forward into her surgery and treatment. I felt astonished at the depth of hope I heard in her voice. It was in that same conversation that she also told me, "I'm going to die eventually from something, but I'm not going to let this illness have my life—my living—now."

That night, something amazing happened as those girls and I got ready for bed. One of them, a quiet fourteen-year-old, had been crying in another room when one of the other girls found her and came to tell me about it. What moved me most was the genuine concern and compassion that all of the other girls instantly showed for her. It turned out that her mother was also battling cancer, and this girl felt sad to be away from her mom and family during such a difficult time.

I was amazed at what remarkable answers my friend's prayers were already bringing as the group of us spontaneously began a long heart-to-heart that eventually ended in its own circle of prayers for her mother, my sister, and all of us. As such conversations often do when the participants are youths, this one included lots of questions, and I think our hearts found many answers that night in our little shared circle. Surprisingly, we all fell asleep peacefully, myself included, and I passed a far better night than I ever would have expected.

The next morning I woke from a dream in which masses of pink bougainvillea blossoms filled up the side of a wall. It left me with a pleasant sense of calm, a shift in my inner numbness, and better energy with which to begin the long day ahead of me, the one during which my sister would undergo surgery. I still felt some wistfulness about my being powerless to help, and I wished there were some tangible way to show her my love and care, especially because I couldn't do it in person.

When I saw my friend at breakfast, I suddenly remembered that she had once lived in the Caribbean. Within hours I was in her studio searching through several dozen paintings. Though beautiful, none were what I sought.

Then I asked her about bougainvillea, and she found a painting that had been hidden away out of sight. The image's familiarity instantly took my breath away. It was a view of a cascade of brilliant pink blooms tumbling over a whitewashed wall—just like the one in my dream, and just like the wall near my sister's deck. In that moment, I was overwhelmed with tears for many reasons, but the biggest was astonished gratitude.

Today that painting is a bright reminder on my sister's wall of the blossoms that did thrive after all, the ones she lived to see and appreciate all the more deeply. For me, it's a reminder that no matter

43

what is happening in our lives, prayer and giving to others are the most precious resources, not because they make the problems go away, but because they change our experience and our perceptions within them. And they do bring answers, though they may not be the ones we think we're looking for.

Some Pennies Just Might Be from Heaven

God's grace, and its answers to our most heartfelt prayers,
is often closer to us than our own pulse and heartbeat.

For nearly twenty years my father has had a pattern of heading south when the weather turns cold, like so many other birds of "the Greatest Generation." As soon as the leaves start taking on autumn colors, he packs up his car with its Florida license plate, dodges the worst of the hurricane season, and makes his way back to the land of orange groves and flamingos.

But this year was different. While there were fewer meteorological monsters to worry about, he's been battling his own personal storm— cancer—the one that has changed so many of his plans lately. For the first time in my adult life, Dad has stuck around in New England long enough to see autumn arrive.

While the future looks uncertain, I couldn't help remembering a little miracle that occurred five years ago, shortly after my mother died unexpectedly. Without his companion of six decades, Dad was the very embodiment of sadness. Within a week of her death, he collapsed and was hospitalized. When I flew down to see him, I knew that, regardless of his illness, he was really fighting to find the will to live and might not succeed. He became increasingly unresponsive, and my heart sank heavier each day.

I remember saying prayers one night that smacked of desperation—I was pleading and even outright bargaining. I also remember fearing that I was going to lose my father before I'd even begun to thaw from the numbness I felt from my mother's death. Lying helplessly in his hospital bed, Dad seemed as far away from me as she did, and I felt very alone.

When I could finally allow my thoughts to quiet a bit that night, I felt a sensation like a soft hand placed briefly on my shoulder, then experienced a feeling similar to what I'd felt in the past when my mother would so often urge me, "Come on, Pet. It'll be all right," whenever I'd shared my troubles with her.

That feeling allowed me to finally go to sleep. That night, I had a dream in which I was standing in the doorway of my father's hospital bathroom, watching as he stood at the sink with his back to me. Someone was standing behind him, much the way a nurse would do, to steady and support him. When I looked in the mirror over the sink, I saw that it was my mother who was standing behind him. Her eyes immediately looked up and gazed back at me before the dream ended.

The next morning, when I went to see Dad at the hospital, a nurse stopped me on my way to his room to inform me that he had gotten up in the night without assistance and, fortunately, made his way to the bathroom without incident. While she was unhappy about his method, she was obviously glad to share news of his improved condition after he'd lain immobile in bed for nearly two weeks. He had also taken not one, but two walks that morning, she told me.

If my expression was one of astonishment, Dad's was one of ecstasy when I came upon him sitting up in his room. He couldn't wait to tell me about his "coup" of getting up and walking all that way. He hadn't actually wanted to do it at first, he told me, but "your mother simply insisted, and so I just had to comply."

After he'd said those words, he looked a bit abashed, as though he regretted letting them out, in case I'd think he was crazy. I'm sure I must have looked a little dazed, standing there staring at him with my mouth open.

We've never spoken of it since, although over the last five years he periodically mentions curious little coincidences that help me feel that my mother is near, and leave him absolutely assured that she is.

When I remember that incident, I'm reminded of the assurance Bahá'u'lláh offers us that God's love and assistance, like a "fathomless and surging Ocean," is "near, astonishingly near, unto you. Behold it is closer to you than your life-vein! Swift as the twinkling of an eye ye can, if ye but wish it, reach and partake of this imperishable favor, this God-given grace, this incorruptible gift, this most potent and unspeakably glorious bounty."[1]

When Dad recently faced an especially scary doctor's appointment, I prayed that he would feel assurance, which, for him, means feeling that my mother is close. As we were gathering up his things to head out, his eye caught a gleaming object on the carpet in his living room and he stooped to retrieve it. He was delighted to discover it was a penny, something that my mother, like many people, always considered a sign of good luck.

But this penny, or "pence," had Queen Elizabeth on the front—like those his English wife had so often carried in her pocket. Dad hadn't seen one around the house for years, and heaven knows where it came from. I do know that it never left his pocket from the time he found it.

Don't Let Them Get Caught without a Prayer

The degree of faith we have in prayer seems to have a direct bearing on the flow of its blessings and on our ability to see them.

Each year, as I embark on the annual fast that is a part of Bahá'í life, I take a spiritual inventory and try to be more conscious about asking for help. I'm talking about the big kind of help here, what some of us call prayer. One friend's creative first response when prayer is suggested is to loudly shout the word "Help!" as she turns imploringly toward the sky.

My husband and I tried to connect our children with this vital resource from the moment we first held them. Our daughter, when she was still just a toddler, had surgery for a birth defect. After the surgery she returned from the recovery room swathed in medical tubing, looking lost in a cage-like crib that prevented us from reaching or touching her.

"Please say prayers," her tiny, post-anesthesia voice croaked as we hung over her, feeling helpless. She was not quite three and already knew exactly what to do first in any uncertain situation.

When her younger brother came along, we whispered prayers into his tiny ears, just as we had with her. Both children also saw our own prayers as a part of daily life. I remember often telling my children, "Thank you for being quiet now. Mummy is praying," and they quickly learned how important it was to have some time alone to pray.

I thought I had a firm grip on what it means to pray, but one day twenty years ago our small son showed me that using prayer and having confidence in it are very different things. It was a wintry March, and I was driving an exciting sports car that my husband's brother had loaned to us while our own car was in the shop. As I was driving to pick up our son at his preschool, it started to snow. At first it was just a pretty coating on the trees, but by the time I reached his school, wet snow was coming down fast and had covered the roads.

I picked up our son, and as we pulled away from the school, our seatbelts safely fastened, the big racing tires on that car sent us into a frightening spin. After I regained control, I realized that it was going to be very difficult to drive home on twisting roads that day. I was scared. I remember saying something out loud that was surely a prayerful plea, probably a lot like my friend's quick-on-the-draw, one-word shout for help.

In the rearview mirror, I saw my son fold his hands, drop his head, and remain silent during that twenty-minute crawl that usually only took ten. When we reached our driveway, he released a large exhalation of relief, looked up at me, and asked, "Is it OK to stop praying now?"

I looked at him, speechless, and realized that this was what he'd been doing as I'd struggled to get us home safely. And of course, his five-year-old's literal logic simply knew that those prayers had done their job, right?

I nodded, still dazed, as I thanked him.

The prayer he had used is one that many Bahá'ís throughout the world employ when faced with challenges: "Is there any Remover of difficulties save God? Say: Praised be God! He is God! All are His servants, and all abide by His bidding!"[2]

This was a somewhat long prayer for such a small soul to have committed to memory. He referred to it at the time as the "e-mover."

The next day, we were out on errands together when I discovered that I'd parked the car over a patch of black ice that made the wheels spin uselessly when I tried to back out of the parking space. Hearing my sigh of frustration, my son again folded his hands and bowed his head without a word.

As I watched him in some amazement, a bright-yellow sand truck turned the corner and stopped beside the car. The driver climbed out, fetched a shovel from the side, scooped some sand out of the truck, and spread it on either side of the car's tires without a word. Stunned, I at least had the presence of mind to roll down the window and thank him before he drove away. My son looked up from his silent entreaty, flashed a huge smile, and said, "Prayer really works, huh? Now we can go!"

Of course, prayer is also more than asking for help. Today my son often combines making music, sketching, and journaling with his prayers and communion with God. Prayer is what he still turns to when he feels in need of help or guidance, or if he simply feels the desire to feed his spirit. That five-year-old's faith in prayer has been with him ever since those icy winter days twenty years ago when he experienced it to be so literally effective.

My husband and I still pray for our children (now grown) every day, and they know this. But of more assurance to my mother's heart is that they learned early on that everything benefits when prayer is applied to it. They know that prayer and the answer that is promised if we pray can come in many forms and that every answer, whatever its outward appearance, is a blessing.

What my son taught me on those wintry days is that the degree of faith we have in prayer has a direct bearing on the flow of those blessings and on our ability to see them.

Listening for Heaven, Even on Earth

Even as my body's sensations echoed this inner awe of my heart, a portion of me stood apart like an observer and thought: "What on earth is this?" Nothing earthly at all, it would seem.

I woke up one recent morning with a prayer running through my head. From the very first moments of a day that begins this way, it's as though I've already experienced happiness all day long. Sometimes it even feels as though I've been experiencing happiness forever. That's the timeless gift of such spiritual grace.

Instead of finding myself awash in thoughts already run rampant, or consciousness dragging to life like sluggish motor oil, here was this mild, steady, comforting rhythm already oscillating inside me— beautiful, all-embracing, transporting.

This affected me so deeply that when it came time to read the prayers I customarily take time to say with my husband each morning, my voice broke with emotion. The mere sight of words making reference to "the All-Merciful, the Compassionate, the Ever-Forgiving" and "the ocean of Thy nearness" overwhelmed me with an awed, ecstatic immersion in something large and welcoming, like an ocean of light.

And even as this happened, and my body's sensations echoed this inner awe of my heart, a portion of me stood apart like an observer and thought, "What on earth is this?"

Nothing earthly at all, it would seem.

I had a pretty good idea as to why I found myself embarking on a new day in this way. I was currently in the midst of what Bahá'ís sometimes call the "Season of Restraint." This is a period at the close of our calendar year when, for nineteen days, we are asked to undergo a material fast from food and drink during daylight hours as "an outer token of the spiritual fast . . . the withholding of oneself from all appetites of the self, taking on the characteristics of the spirit, being carried away by the breathings of heaven and catching fire from the love of God."[3]

Fasting from the appetites of the body reminds us of how insistent these can be, of course. And how much time the business of survival can consume in our day, especially when it's overemphasized to the point at which we might forget that we have a spiritual life at all. A reprieve from giving so much attention to these things leaves more time for the seeking and partaking of spiritual nourishment—prayer and reflection, imbibing spiritual guidance, and listening and observing for the many ways in which spirituality wafts into our lives.

In the course of such activities, I found myself increasingly attracted to the word "relinquish" whenever it appeared before me in prayers and passages. I found myself considering both restraint and relinquishment and began to discover how intimately related they can be. A search for synonyms for "restraint" yields words and phrases such as "self-control," "self-discipline," and "moderation." Another descriptor that really appealed to me was "self-possession." Does this imply true possession of one's self? I wondered.

Whereas restraint seems like a condition that arises from my taking responsibility for my self and actions, "relinquish" means to surrender or hand over. It almost makes the two sound like opposites—or maybe complementary partners.

Surrender and handing over can be very tall orders, of course. But the list also included two other synonyms that sound like accessible first steps in that process: "let go by" and "let pass." While endeavoring to practice genuine restraint, in a spiritual sense, what I suddenly heard in the possibility of relinquishment was an invitation to freedom—a letting go of the erroneous notions and occasional tyranny of my own thoughts.

Now, I'm not talking about the presence-of-mind thoughts we experience when engaged in focused, constructive effort. I'm talking about the ones that spin round and round, either in the past or in the presumed future. They usually suggest unhelpful things and never, ever, take me anywhere new. Noise, some might call it.

Each morning as I said my daily prayers and encountered all of these references to relinquishment, it suddenly occurred to me, here in this season of restraint, that there was something well worth restraining or moderating—my thoughts.

And how does one restrain or moderate his or her thoughts? By letting your thoughts go by as they arise. And by spending time in prayer, spiritual study, and reflection—something that can lead to waking up with a taste of heaven and feeling that flood of grace that is poured out in every moment for our sake.

In a book called *The Seven Valleys and The Four Valleys*, Bahá'u'lláh writes, "A servant is drawn unto Me in prayer until I answer him; and when I have answered him, I become the ear wherewith he heareth. . . ."[4]

When we relinquish something lesser for something greater, we seem to catch the sweet notes of that higher kind of hearing. As insistent as our thoughts can be, it seems that when we're willing to relinquish them and, especially their insistence, what appears in place of them feels positively eternal.

It makes me a little wistful to think that by the time this column appears, this season will be behind me. I'll have broken this fast and celebrated Naw-Rúz—the joyful arrival of the new Bahá'í year at the vernal equinox.

But like one who's had a taste of water in the desert, or of freedom after imprisonment, I find that my encounter with the grace in relinquishment has brought with it a sense of promise, an imprint of the everlasting—an emblem of hope that sheds light on the path in front of me. It feels like a little bit of heaven on earth, visible through the window of each and every moment.

CHAPTER 4

UNTO HIM SHALL WE RETURN

"And now concerning thy question regarding the soul of man and its survival after death. Know thou of a truth that the soul, after its separation from the body, will continue to progress until it attaineth the presence of God, in a state and condition which neither the revolution of ages and centuries, nor the changes and chances of this world, can alter. It will endure as long as the Kingdom of God, His sovereignty, His dominion and power will endure. It will manifest the signs of God and His attributes, and will reveal His loving kindness and bounty."

—Bahá'u'lláh, *Gleanings from the Writings of Bahá'u'lláh*

A Life with Room for Dying

In those places where people, and those who loved them, were feeling the approach of something so large and unknown as death, beyond the fear and pain, the struggle and sadness, there was always another feeling of something truly akin to peace.

As a nurse, in younger days, I gained privileged access to two very significant transitions in human life. I was immersed in the otherworldly atmosphere that accompanies a meeting of worlds at every birth. And I witnessed in humbled awe how very similar the atmosphere could be in a room where someone was on his way out of this life.

Of course, we're all on our way out eventually. We've been drawing closer to death and farther from the newness of life ever since we arrived. But in those places where people, and those who loved them, were feeling the approach of something so large and unknown as death, beyond the fear and pain, the struggle and sadness, there was always another feeling of something truly akin to peace.

That sense of peace was a lot like the sun, in a way. The sun is always there. Whether we feel it or not depends on what factors there are between it and us—things like clouds, nightfall, or thick walls that admit no light. But the sun is always there, and sometimes it even feels as though its rays come looking for us when we seem to have forgotten about it. Something that I saw in other people's experience with impending death made that same impression on me. There was a sense of a warming, light-filled possibility of something greater than us gently making its presence known.

I hadn't given this much thought until so much in my family's life began to be about living with someone who was dying. This happened when my husband's father and his life's final chapter became a part of our household's daily rhythms. Our conversations increasingly centered on pain management and palliative care, and this man's children gradually became as familiar with medical-care settings as I once had been on a workday basis. We all began to feel as though we'd woken up in someone else's life.

In my days as a nurse I encountered situations I never could have imagined. One was how painful life can feel when some family members are trying to do everything right in order to earn a miracle, while others are endeavoring to make peace with what they know in their hearts isn't going to bring one.

I remember my fellow nurses telling me stories of their encounters with families dealing with death. One I remember very clearly was about a dying woman who simply wanted to take care of some necessary matters on behalf of her children, but whose siblings got angry at her for even bringing it up, as though she were somehow hastening the specter of their worst-case scenario, the passing into which she'd already begun her journey. I can't imagine how very alone she must have felt.

Yet, as the wonderful Bill Moyers' series "Living with Dying" repeatedly reminds, there is no right way to traverse this stage of the journey of life. It's undoubtedly the single biggest thing we all face, with most of us giving it next to no preparation at all.

It's so surprising the kinds of things that come to feel like breakthroughs in this process, like rays of sun reaching in. One was the relief that flooded in when the family member who had been holding out for that miracle could finally share her fear aloud and then let it go. That's when we all discovered what a sweet grace it is when you're there to catch each other at those times when fear and worries grow too large to bear. At that point, you need to hold together and reassure each other that you're all going through it together. The rays of the sun come through very brightly on days like that.

Such days lent new meaning to words of Bahá'u'lláh that I have carried in my heart for a long time: "O Son of the Supreme! I have made death a messenger of joy to thee. Wherefore dost thou grieve? I made the light to shed on thee its splendor. Why dost thou veil thyself therefrom?"[1]

Why, indeed, do we veil ourselves from that light? Sadly, it's what we seem to do in a culture that fears death and dying much the way our ancestors ran and hid from events in the night sky that they couldn't explain.

Yet, increasingly, there are those who do not run from it, or have learned how not to. Just when my family most needed those courageous individuals who seem at peace with death, they seemed to cross our path and reach out to us with the informed, compassionate perspective of those who have consciously and actively engaged in the spiritual process of a loved one's dying.

I notice that they are people with soft eyes (perhaps softer now than they used to be) who move in an atmosphere of trusting contentment that allows them to offer so much to others simply through their presence. The experience of meeting death with an awareness of the light that surrounds it is what has brought them to this place of acceptance. It's also what proved an invaluable assistance as they met the inevitable grief they felt in the aftermath.

That gentle light that seems to envelop the atmosphere during the passing of a loved one has so much to offer us, they told me. It's what helps us remember that joy and pain can and do exist simultaneously in this life, and that life feels more whole when we can accept that. We can then experience more completely that aspect of ourselves that remains unaffected by either, the part that will move on, in time, just like those loved ones to whom we're saying good-bye, for now.

Through the insight of souls like these who welcome that light, my sister-in-law and I, who previously hardly knew each other, are each coming to recognize that our family is indeed receiving a miracle, even if it's not one of medical healing. It is the daily increasing love affair of siblings from two separate families coming to know, love, and help each other in ways they never could have predicted. It is my father-in-law's dearest wish coming true before his eyes.

The Gift of a Winter's Grace

Like birth, so much about the process of death can be orderly,
purposeful, and quite wondrous by design.

One day, some years ago, I watched as a family sat companionably together in a small sitting area outside the room where their loved one had just died. Their circle had an unhurried and inviting calm as they talked quietly together. The atmosphere around them, which occasionally included a peal of soft laughter, was irresistibly attractive. I hovered like a moth near this group that seemed so utterly at peace. When they graciously invited me over, I immediately felt the intensity of the light and warmth around them.

Today I understand just what they were doing and what attracted me. They were imbibing a kind of aftermath, one in which they were deliberately extending their experience of a connection with something greater than themselves, and with each other, before they had to go their separate ways again. They were basking in the quiet awe that results from their having witnessed together someone's last breaths, and their having accompanied him as he found his final freedom.

The setting was a nearly new hospice house in Massachusetts. My husband's family had just arrived there that afternoon after learning that my father-in-law would be spending his last days and hours there, and that there weren't likely to be many more of them. We were all still taking it in, feeling a bit as though we were in a dream, yet very grateful to know that this unexpected oasis had somehow appeared on the horizon, both for his sake and for ours.

Our relief was a kind of gasping, breathless astonishment. We hadn't even known how much pain we'd been in until we were suddenly granted this chance to have capable, incredibly caring hands take over. The preceding weeks had been ones of increasing pain for this man who was suffering from cancer, and hours of hopeless anguish for the rest of us as we'd repeatedly encountered how very little we were able to do to assist him any further.

In those first few hours after we settled into this new "home," we were in a sort of psychic culture shock. It was as though we'd all been clinging together on a small raft in the midst of the ocean, watching a storm build as the waves rose higher and higher, and wondering when the end would finally engulf us. Then, suddenly, it was as if we'd awakened on a luxurious ocean liner where the first and unquestioned priority was to take care of all of us. I think we must have felt a bit like foundlings that day, and finally seeing our loved one get a reprieve from his pain stirred very deep feelings of gratitude within us. We were still afraid, sad, and uncertain, but we were coming to believe that there really was a kinder—and more life-affirming—way toward the end after all, and that hospice is a very benevolent and competent custodian on that path.

Like birth, so much about the process of death can be orderly, purposeful, and quite wondrous by design. I can see now why some have likened it to a physical birth in reverse. Knowledge is a source of empowerment and reassurance as one watches this process, and it's remarkable how hospice imparts precisely the information that families need in order to understand more fully what happens when it's time to say good-bye to someone and to let go of whatever fear is still being held inside. Hospice's own profound understanding of the process of death also facilitates the utmost physical comfort possible for the patient.

We miss so much of life by avoiding contact with death. In six days that held more than many months ever could, my family and I came to know a level of awe, love, and joy that we hadn't imagined possible when facing a loved one's death. The beauty and intimacy in accompanying someone on his final progression toward death, and making that journey together as a family, is an experience that still moves us to tears. It truly defies any words or description.

In 1911 'Abdu'l-Bahá was asked, "How should one look forward to death?" He replied, "How does one look forward to the goal of any journey? With hope and with expectation. It is even so with the end of this earthly journey."[2]

An awful lot of Americans are going to die over the next thirty to forty years, in part because so very many of us have been born since the Second World War. Those of us who were born in the 1950s and '60s have seen the birth experience brought back from sterile, isolated settings into the more homelike, human dimension in which loved ones can share in the wonder of welcoming a new little soul. And, at last, the wisdom of the hospice movement is helping us reclaim and embrace death as a part of life meant to be shared and accompanied by loved ones, too.

Yet despite decades of dedicated work by people like Elisabeth Kübler-Ross, who was the author of a number of groundbreaking books about death and dying, there still seems to be a huge, hands-off taboo when it comes to dying, something I'm beginning to think might be making many of us ill even while we're living.

My family probably will never be able to thank the attentive doctor sufficiently or fully appreciate the remarkably good timing that helped my husband's dad receive the gift of a bed in a hospice house, rare as they are in these times. Clichéd as it may sound, every encounter we had with hospice from our very first contact, like the logo on the local hospice sign, was like a lighthouse guiding us safely to shore. When we reached the refuge of the hospice house itself, it was as though dozens of pairs of caring arms had caught us up in a safe haven.

Because of those gifts, there were five of us in the room when the final moments came, and that room had truly come to feel like home for us all. My father-in-law was surrounded by the family members who had been caring for him in the previous months. His daughters and son held him and talked with him quietly, comforting him and telling him that they loved him and that it was OK to take that step, even as we all cried freely when they spoke those words. It took perhaps a minute, and then, with a gentle sigh and a small smile at the end, he was gone. It was one of many sweet, tender moments that have been a part of this journey.

We were all amazed and quite grateful. And like that family I'd seen the week before, we lingered together in that soft, light-kissed atmosphere in an unhurried way before we returned to the lives that were waiting for us.

From the time of his diagnosis, my father-in-law lived about the length of the winter, a fitting metaphor for his final stage in this life. I think that those of us who held him in those last moments can all feel within us the very breath of spring toward which he was reaching next.

My Father's New Garden

*While the pain of physical separation remains for
those left behind, for the one who dies, it's as though a
wise gardener has transplanted a struggling plant to
a place where it can reach a new level of growth.*

The rooms of my father's house are an empty canvas now. The old carpeting has been uprooted and torn away, the walls washed over in a clean mask of white.

Yet if I listen closely, I can still hear the echoes of his hours here in the weeks before he left this place for the last time: the television's blare to an empty room, the dying shriek of the kettle forgotten on the stove, the mindless beep of an answering machine that received only prerecorded sales calls. I can see the unmade bed and crowded sink—and the dwindling pile of mail.

It's not because this house is so empty now that it pained me to come inside. It's that near the end of his life it was so empty even when he was still living here.

For the past twenty-six years my summer calendar has included the many visits I had with my parents when they returned from Florida to their summer home in Maine. For the past six and a half years those occasions included only my dad, and I tried to ensure that there were more of them each week, since my mother's death meant that he was on his own during those intervals in between.

Three years ago things took a major turn when he was diagnosed with cancer. And over the last year, whatever relationship I thought I had with time was blurred into that suspended state you live in when someone you love has a terminal illness.

Last fall it became obvious that my father could no longer live in his house alone, no matter how strong his assertions otherwise. There was absolutely nothing easy about that transition. If it hadn't been for the help of an insightful doctor and a number of social workers and advisers, it wouldn't have happened—and it needed to. And even though it afforded him a much-improved living situation afterward, I still wound up feeling like a culprit or accomplice.

Last month I had the chance to see just how wonderful that new living situation had been for him. After four months of life there, months that had been far more companionable than any hours in his deteriorating home could ever have been, he entered the final weeks of his life. As I kept him company, I had the privilege of watching a dozen staff members come in to take tender care of him and to wish him well on his journey. During that final week, these folks who had truly come to love him mirrored back to him his own virtues of generosity and kindness. I believe they were the ones who really helped him to "pack his spiritual bags." There were days when I couldn't tell whether I was crying more for my own loss or for theirs.

There was grace for me, as well, through the agency of hospice's help, and I was sitting right beside my dad on the bed when he took his last breaths. My hand was on his heart as we sent him off with love and praise for the very brave job he had followed through to the very end.

A stubborn Irishman to the core, my father would never have openly admitted that the facility to which he'd moved had brought the right balance of care and companionship that he had truly needed. But I think that, in his way, he showed me the truth of this during that final week. I do know that I've felt less like a culprit since.

When I was finally able to visit his now-empty house again, I felt comforted (and accompanied) as I moved about its rooms, quietly reciting prayers, making my final farewells.

Then I looked out the sliders at the back and was nearly bowled over by the brilliance of what was waiting there. Every bush and shrub he'd planted over the years seemed to be in bloom at once, as if in blatant testimony to the indomitable strength of nature and life itself.

All of the beautiful plants in bloom reminded me of that last bit of gardening we'd done together the year before. Dad had a little strip of land against the back of his house in which he'd plant impatiens every year. Last June I'd spied two big trays of them on his back patio and realized that, since he could barely walk any longer, there was no way he could plant these himself.

We were quite a team that day, the two of us—plus his ever-eager miniature schnauzer, Patsy, namesake of the saint on whose day she was born. In our curious assembly line, Dad churned up the soil in the beds with a long-handled trowel and I followed behind, nestling the little plants into place. It had just rained, so the job was messy, the mosquitoes thick, and Patsy determined to be right in my face as I hunkered over those beds.

But I knew even then that the task was going to be one of the very last things we'd do together. And, with nature's benevolence, the flowers were still there long into the fall. As soon as I'd remembered them, I knew what we'd need for Dad's funeral.

His funeral service was an event fit for the Irishman he was. His all-time favorite waitress from his favorite restaurant gave a moving tribute to the man she called "my oldest friend, and the one who convinced me not to give up on love. And I've finally found it," she said as she held up the new ring on her finger.

My brother-in-law recalled asking Dad for my sister's "hand" eleven years before, to which his future father-in-law had replied with his customary whimsy, "Go ahead, take all of her. I gave her away, but she keeps coming back."

My husband recalled our eight-year-old son solemnly watching Grampie put together an outdoor grill and being too polite to tell him that he'd assembled a few of its parts upside down. My father had laughed about his grandson's "diplomacy" for years afterward.

After we'd given Dad the best tribute we could, there were little flats of impatiens waiting outside for each guest to take home to plant, since my father wouldn't be gardening this year. I've already had calls from friends and family in four states saying how much they loved the idea of watching those little flowers, reminders of my father, bloom far and wide this summer.

I can't take any credit for this idea. Sending folks home with flowers was the essence of what my father himself would have done. I know he planted that thought as I was wandering around his condo for the last time, right after he'd made sure that I'd noticed the profusion of blooming glory out back.

In a passage very dear to me, 'Abdu'l-Bahá counsels someone who has experienced the loss of a loved one that, while the pain of physical separation remains for those left behind, for the one who dies, it's as though a wise and kind gardener has transplanted a struggling plant to a wider, more welcoming place where it can reach a whole new level of growth. I know my father is out there somewhere, growing and blooming to his full potential.

A Balm for Every Wound

"One for each of you," I can hear my mother say as I recall
her deep resolve to always treat her two daughters fairly.

I'm amazed at how instantly I've recognized my father each time he
appears lately. When I've spotted him on narrow European streets,
and gleaming dance floors, across which he guided me as a child years
ago, I've immediately had a strong, sensory recollection of the way
the skin on his cheek and hand feel, and the breadth of his shoulders
when I put my arm around them. In these recent encounters, those
shoulders are, once again, broader and better padded than they were
when I touched them a year ago, not long before he died.

The nighttime visits of these dreams have become very matter-
of-fact for me, as down-to-earth and straightforward as my father
himself tended to be. They feel so concrete that when I enclose him
in a sturdy hug, or kiss his cheek—knowing full well, as I do, that
he's no longer living in this same physical world that I am—the
experience feels as solid and real in my memory afterward as it does
during these affectionate reunions that take place in my dreams.

In each dream he comforts me with his presence and I respond with
reassuring words about how I know, deep down, that all is well with
him and with me. True to his personality, my father doesn't surprise me
with these visits so much as follow through on what I would expect.

My mother, however, is a whole other matter. Without a doubt,
she had an enigmatic, quicksilver personality and loved the element
of surprise too much not to wield it as best she could, even from
beyond this world.

I know that my parents, each in his or her very own style, have
been close over this last month. That's in part because when my sister,
my only other family member, had surgery recently, she was quite
fearful. She told me that she'd been dealing with a host of dreads and
demons as the surgery date approached, one of which was the terror
that she wouldn't wake up afterward.

This was her second journey through the experience of cancer. I
asked an ever-widening circle of souls for prayers on her behalf. I,

of course, said many prayers for her too, one of which was that she would feel our parents' love close to her. The last time she walked this road a little more than ten years ago, Mum and Dad had gone to be with her almost as soon as they received news of her illness and stayed with her through the days of her surgery.

So I made my prayerful request, and there was Dad, dropping by between the end of one day and the start of the next. "Why are you showing up here?" I wanted to ask afterward. But then I remembered that the way my father tended to try to connect with my sister was usually through me.

Then I turned once again to the boxes of my father's belongings I've been working my way through as I find the emotional strength to do so. They were shipped from his Florida home, and my passage through each, brimming as it is with a veritable Pharaoh's tomb of feelings and memories, is no small challenge. If nothing else, my father's nocturnal visits have left me feeling a bit psychically nagged about these containers of his belongings.

Suddenly, as I was unpacking one day, there my mother was, between a framed photograph of a British relative and one of my father's journals. The image of her face gazed back at me from a misty cloud, as though looking in from a world beyond. This was clearly a "mistake" in the photograph, a double-exposure, perhaps.

But its effect was somehow timely and pertinent—and there was another just like it stuck to the back. "One for each of you," I could immediately hear my mother say, whether in my imagination or in actuality I can't be sure. The tone of her voice to my inner ear was real enough, as real as her resolve always was to treat her two daughters fairly.

Then, in the next layer of the box were four folded pieces of stationery with her writing on them. As I looked closely, I saw that the pages contained a list of her recollections of family life from the time my sister was four or five years old, a period in which she and my parents had lived in France and Germany shortly after World War II.

The warmth and wit—and unmistakable love—in my mother's voice was alive on those little pages. By the next day, they were folded around one of those photos of my mother and on their way to my sister by mail, her very own one-of-a-kind "visit."

And the day that I mailed it out, my sister learned that her surgeon had given her the "all clear" for cancer. How about that?

I was struck yet again by the individuality of the way in which each of us reaches out with love to others, whether in this world or beyond it; whether in a more pragmatic, time-to-unpack-the-boxes way, like my father, or my mother's time-transcending message that still showed her love for surprises.

I was also reminded how very subtle and beautiful the responses to prayer can be, almost like hummingbird sightings or shooting stars. All too easily missed if we're too distracted by the clamor of life around us.

CHAPTER 5

THE TRANQUILLITY OF NATIONS

"The well-being of mankind, its peace and security, are unattainable unless and until its unity is firmly established."

—Bahá'u'lláh, *Gleanings from the Writings of Bahá'u'lláh*

The Same Winds Blow on Us All

World peace is not only possible but inevitable.
It is the next stage in the evolution of this planet.

There's a game I used to like to play with large groups back in my conference-planning days because of its fast-acting ability to bring a large and diverse group of people together. It's called "The West Wind Blows," and it involves getting players to sit in chairs arranged in a circle while one person in the middle calls out different descriptors such as "The West Wind blows on everybody wearing socks" or "The West Wind blows on everyone who's ever gone skiing." If the description applies to you, you stand up and scurry to another place in the circle.

In order to be a good sport and keep things lively, you have to move out of the "safe" comfort zone of simply swapping places with someone next to you and strike out into the circle itself. If the chairs are all filled before you find a new one, you get the privilege of being the one in the middle trying to think up the next description until you're able to rush to an empty seat again.

At its best, this game keeps everyone moving around, often for quite some time, and just about all ages can play it together. Within minutes, this game can weld a diverse group of fifty adults and children into a bustling, giggling mass of happy people all focused on the same thing. It's a game that gives everyone permission to let down their barriers and just enjoy themselves.

As many games do, it also offers opportunities to model or reinforce positive behaviors. You have to cooperate and pay attention. You have to move skillfully and quickly while also being considerate and careful of others' movements.

If the game is to be really enjoyable, it absolutely has to avoid becoming competitive. In groups that can include grandparents, teens, children, parents, and toddlers, it usually doesn't take long before big people start helping the very small ones and kids suddenly start giving up their seat to an elder or peer who's having trouble getting out of the middle. (Not that being in the middle is such a bad thing.)

The variation and balance of similarities and differences is what seems key in this game, what keeps everyone attentive, and what ensures that all will be included. Curiously, your best chance at getting out of the middle is to be as inclusive as possible. The greater the number of people you get up and moving, the greater your chances of finding a chair—and the more fun everyone has. You might say that inclusiveness is the game's objective, and the way you reach it is by focusing on how much more similar we are than different.

As I played the game again recently, the analogy of what a very good model it is for being inclusive in our actions—whether in families, our community, at work, or at play—was too obvious to miss.

A coming together of the world's peoples in a relationship as harmonious, open, and welcoming as a good game of "The West Wind Blows" is clearly a need of our times, if a far more complex prospect. There seems to be little doubt that creating such a universal culture of collaboration and conciliation will require great effort on our part.

The job is big, the tasks complex, and many of the elements quite daunting. But the promise is big, and the reward unprecedented if we can find the wisdom and will to embrace the diversity of the world, which is truly a gift from God, and let it be the path to unity.

In 1985 the international governing body of the Bahá'í Faith, the Universal House of Justice, wrote a statement on world peace that promises, "World peace is not only possible but inevitable. It is the next stage in the evolution of this planet."[1]

The statement cautions, "Whether peace is to be reached only after unimaginable horrors precipitated by humanity's stubborn clinging to old patterns of behavior, or is to be embraced now by an act of consultative will, is the choice before all who inhabit the earth."[2]

Unity is our ultimate destination. As Bahá'u'lláh reminds, "The well-being of mankind, its peace and security, are unattainable unless and until its unity is firmly established. . . . Deal ye one with another with the utmost love and harmony, with friendliness and fellowship."[3]

And, lest we forget, feel frustrated, or think this gift from God may not be achievable in our time, it helps to remember the darkness it will dispel: "So powerful is the light of unity that it can illuminate the whole earth."[4]

No matter what kinds of winds may blow on us, or how hard, it does appear that we'll benefit far more by facing them together as a unified group, discovering what we all have in common, rather than as individuals focusing on all of our minor differences.

Culture-Shocked, and Learning to Like It

*Culture shock often interrupts those things we do reflexively
and haven't spent much time thinking about—yet.*

Whether we travel or not, I think everyone eventually experiences some form of culture shock, the shift in perspective that results from our being out of our usual surroundings.

Experiencing a new culture begins with a honeymoon quality in which things are pleasantly new and different, like the time my friend's children, born in Holland where they don't have fire hydrants, wondered what these curious objects were when they first saw them on American streets.

Culture shock's challenge looms when we discover that the familiar framework on which we depend unthinkingly each day is suddenly gone. In its place is a foreign landscape for which we have no map and no guide to the rules that govern proper behavior. Or the rules may contradict the way we think things should be. When I lived and worked in China, small tasks became mountains because I couldn't do anything reflexively, especially without knowing the language. There were times when I also had to fight off a nagging insistence that the way I knew was better.

My friend later visited her son, the youngest of those kids who hadn't seen fire hydrants, where he was living as a young adult in Minsk, the capital of Belarus. She was shocked when his girlfriend described how, following her art teacher's suggestion, she had visited a new hotel's dig site and found a human skull that she brought out to sketch before reburying it later.

"What was she doing? That is *awful,*" was my friend's first thought. Fortunately, the three of them talked about it. As a seasoned world traveler, she's encountered culture shock too often to stop at her first morally outraged reaction.

The young artist had replied, "But our city is *built* on blood and bones," an eloquent summary of the horrific adversity that is Russia's legacy.

"When I heard that, I remembered that I've no right to judge someone whose life I don't live," my friend said. Then she described how the three of them had gone out to the bus stop where, when the sun dropped low, the girl had moved to stand in front of my friend.

"She'd automatically shielded me from the sun," my friend recalled. "I'd have missed such subtle kindness if I'd been caught up in judging her behavior."

Being in another culture simply accelerates our opportunity to experience those periodic cycles of upheaval that, while difficult, are often the means that lead to the most learning and growth. I experienced that in an unexpected way when our two grown children were home in our house for the first time in three years. When I learned that our daughter would return home from China, I knew she was in for some culture shock. I also knew it was going to be a time of adjustment for all of us.

At first, I relished the early honeymoon stage as the four of us enjoyed quality time together again. Then I collided with what inevitably develops when people come together with their acquired habits and expectations.

"What's wrong with the dryer?" I asked upon discovering the bathroom festooned with wet clothes one morning.

Our daughter, who had done laundry without a dryer for the past three years, informed me she had absolutely no intention of submitting clothes purchased with her own money to an environmentally unfriendly machine that invariably shrinks and wears them out faster.

I took a breath, realizing that this is as reasonable a view to her as any I might have. Her brother soon strung a clothesline outside to clear away the clothes that were taking over the bathroom, and we began saving on electricity, too.

Next, it began to seem as though every application and form, anything our daughter had to deal with, had to be dispatched immediately.

"Can't this wait until I've had my coffee, first? Must we run out this minute?" I'd plead.

When we talked, I was reminded that in China there's no "future." People seldom make plans for next week. What you have is today, and windows of opportunity close fast. If you don't seize your chance, you may not get another. This had been our daughter's cultural reality for some of the fullest—and most recent—years of her life.

I'm glad I stepped back and made time to talk rather than simply react to her behavior. Mutual understanding can be a great stress-reducer. Plus, this same culturally influenced bent of hers is also what prompts her to make thoughtful calls from the store on her way home to see whether we need anything.

Culture shock often interrupts those things we usually do almost automatically and haven't spent much time thinking about—yet. Many of my long-time behaviors have been reflexive ones based on what I thought I knew.

Relating to adult children, whether or not you happen to be living with them, is somewhat like encountering a new culture, one that almost seems to require a new language, at times. You can't make assumptions, especially those based solely on your previous experiences with them. Yet with good listening, respectful courtesy, and some willingness to be flexible, you can learn quite a lot about life together.

I never expected to encounter culture shock quite this close to home. I'm glad I had that chance to go half a world away first, so I'd at least know it when I see it.

Cleaning Wives and Warning Labels

In the confounding business of communication, it helps
to remember that people do not always mean exactly what they say.

This summer, for the second year in a row, I seized the opportunity to spend some weeks in Germany, my childhood home. It's partly a homecoming for me and partly a chance to try to advance my determined—if primitive—German-language skills.

And since I'm currently working on a book that's set in Germany as well as America, it was the perfect opportunity to do research while immersed in the very scenes I'm writing about.

My husband and I shared a delightful two weeks of vacation, and then I stayed on in our small vacation-rental apartment for another month. I didn't need an alarm clock, thanks to the symphony of bells from my neighbors, three huge old churches. As my brain seemed to nearly forget English while struggling to grasp another language, I had a number of interesting cross-cultural communication encounters.

Several of these exchanges occurred with my kind landlord. I knew him alternatively as "Wolfgang" or "Herr S." (for Strathausen) as he'd sign off with one or the other in the friendly notes he'd leave so as not to disturb or interrupt me. The more formal sort of address, "Herr Strathausen," is always the safest choice in Germany, although, as he's a bit younger than I, that kind of thing could feel pretty ridiculous, especially for an invariably casual American like me.

He has a plum of a job, if a rather unusual one. He works mainly from home as a software engineer doing the very expensive repair work on those lifelike infant dolls they use in schools now, the ones with computer chips that help them act so much like real babies. So, every once in a while, between the hourly church bells, the sound of the fountain outside my window, and the periodic notice from a cuckoo clock somewhere above me in his part of the house, I would suddenly hear the incongruous sound of a baby's cry or cooing coming from this single man's digs.

Our first verbal exchange concerned when I would like to have the "cleaning wife" come to my rental apartment. I stared back at him in open-mouthed stupor until intuition kicked in and it occurred to me that he might mean "cleaning lady," or "cleaning woman," rather than wife. Indeed, the term in German literally translates to "cleaning wife," but, of course, people do not always mean exactly what they say.

Another interesting exchange happened one afternoon when Herr S. was at my door asking whether I might be able to help him with some English translation. In his hand was a label he'd received with a shipment from the Wisconsin production company he works for. He simply couldn't figure out what it was trying to say and why he would need to know it.

I can only imagine now what this exchange of ours would look like were I to see it recorded on film. The puzzler in question was all of twenty-five words or less. He had never seen one of these labels before that day and was obviously concerned that it might carry some important message for him, and he was frustrated that the message remained elusive because of his limited English.

As I looked at one side of this colorful little banner, I saw that it insisted, "Warning! Do not remove this label!"

Quite naturally, this caused him some consternation, once I'd helped him understand it, because this label clearly wasn't attached to anything anymore.

I tried to reassure him that this was likely just an over-exaggerated bit of unnecessary alarm, a demand as unreasonable as those insistent notes attached to pillows and mattresses.

Then, on its reverse side, in the spirit of the very best technical writing, the label went on to describe how to properly "insert the unit" or "install the component" in question (to which the label presumably comes attached) "inside the device" without the computer chip in the component making contact with the "skin" (presumably the plastic of the doll).

I probably don't need to describe what conveying a concept like this begins to look like when two people must communicate primarily by means of pantomime, gestures, and random words that are understood by both in either German or English—or sometimes a mixture of the two. Two people, that is, who are doing their best, in the confusing waters of not sharing a language, to also be scrupulously and respectfully polite and appropriate.

He was obviously quite confounded by this thing. That was discernible from the continuing contortion of his facial expression in deep worry, and from the way he eventually launched into a long, rapid stream of German, then caught himself suddenly and remembered that he was talking to me, the linguistic equivalent of a German kindergartner—on really good days.

There was only one thing for us to do to solve our language impasse—we had to take that label upstairs to his workshop and study it in the context of the work he does. So we climbed the stairs to the low-beamed space under the eaves of his three-hundred-year-old house, a setting that looks as though Pinocchio might appear in it at any moment. We looked together at the labels and at the dolls until the answer finally became obvious.

It turns out that that label was simply a warning for those un-predictable American customers who can do so many crazy, unpredictable things in our lawsuit-happy world. (Neither "unpredictable" nor "litigious" are common concepts in Herr Strathausen's culture.) It was not, he was relieved to finally realize, an important message for a "specialist" such as he.

My all-time favorite language-related encounter came near the very end of my trip. I was waiting on a train platform when a woman came up and asked the group of people standing next to me whether they knew if the train scheduled for that track would stop in Marburg.

I'd just looked at the itinerary and knew that, yes, in fact, it would. It was the stop right before my own. None of the Germans she approached seemed to respond or help, so I stepped in (feeling a little miffed with them, I have to say) to assure her that, indeed, this train stopped in Marburg. I told her when it was due to depart, about how long the trip to Marburg would take, and when it would arrive there. Then I even led her over to the schedule to boost her confidence, so that she could see with her own eyes that this was the case.

It was only when she thanked me and I turned toward the train as it pulled into the station that I realized what had happened. She had asked for help in English, (quite possibly the reason those she'd approached hadn't been able to offer much more than shrugs or shaking of their heads) and I had confidently proceeded to "help" her entirely in German.

Fortunately, she got on the right train. And hopefully I'll wind up being able to recognize and speak at least one language properly before all this "practice" is over.

The Way Home

*Bahá'u'lláh's invitation to see the Face of the Beloved in
every one of our fellow inhabitants on the planet still extends itself to
all of us, as it did when He walked in the
Holy Land more than a century ago.*

When I made a Bahá'í pilgrimage to Haifa, Israel, last month, I experienced a reunion with my worldwide family, with my own heart, and with the One Whose love is, for me, a generating point of true unity.

The nine-day Bahá'í pilgrimage experience offers followers of Bahá'u'lláh the opportunity to visit those places associated with their Faith's Prophet-Founder during the last half of the 1800s, when He and His family lived in this part of the world as prisoners of the state after various governments, determined to suppress His world-embracing message, exiled Him here from His native Iran. The fact that these prisoners, women and children among them, survived that harsh journey of exile and incarceration at all is a miracle story in itself.

During their pilgrimage, Bahá'ís visit two places on earth that they regard as especially precious. One is the resting place of the Faith's forerunner, known as the Báb (meaning in Arabic the "Gate"), situated under a golden dome on the slopes of Mount Carmel. The other is the pinnacle of pilgrimage for every Bahá'í—reaching the threshold of the Shrine of Bahá'u'lláh Himself, located in the vicinity of the ancient walled city of 'Akká, named for Joan of Arc, where Bahá'u'lláh and His loved ones were imprisoned for nearly a quarter of a century.

Back in the days when Bahá'u'lláh dwelled here, Bahá'í pilgrims walked hundreds of often-dangerous miles from other parts of Asia to reach this place. Usually, they were refused entry at the gate of the city and, standing at a moat outside the citadel that held Him, rejoiced if they chanced to see His hand wave to them through His prison window.

This is the place where much revelation flowed from Bahá'u'lláh's pen, including a proclamation of His divine mission to the political and religious leaders of that day. He urged them to adopt a new vision of worldwide peace and unity, which He described as God's intention for this stage of humanity's spiritual evolution.

Now thousands of fortunate Bahá'í pilgrims offer their prayers from within that prison cell itself, which serves as a tangible reminder that no Messenger of God ever brought a new revelation without suffering cruelty and injustice. Today's Bahá'í pilgrims draw close to every place connected with Bahá'u'lláh's life during His years in the Holy Land before His death in 1892. Not only do they get to visit all of the sacred sites associated with the Bahá'í Faith, they also get to experience a veritable feast of reunion with their fellow pilgrims.

The worldwide Bahá'í family hails from every nation, religious background, and every conceivable social stratum. More than 2,100 ethnic groups and nationalities are represented in the Bahá'í community. World leaders in the time of Bahá'u'lláh may have chosen not to listen to Him, but His message has still managed to reach the hearts of millions of souls around the world.

Today those souls are the fruit, the very lifeblood of His efforts. They have embraced His Message that one God, out of love, created the human family in oneness, and has now, as promised through the ages, provided all the means by which it may be spiritually and materially united. It is a promise that, while asking humanity to accept new guidance from God, also honors every single Messenger that God has sent previously, and values the contribution that each and every soul has to make to that process.

As we strive to accept the invitation Bahá'u'lláh extended to the whole human family, Bahá'ís rely on faith, daily prayer, and meditative study of the sacred texts to bring about the transformation of character necessary for the spiritual maturity that a united world requires. But beyond an experience of personal salvation, we're also seeking to create the kind of civilization that will draw out the spiritual gems treasured in each individual and fashion patterns of unity more powerful than any of the barriers that human minds and cultural assumptions have conceived.

In His writings and teachings, Bahá'u'lláh repeatedly used light as a metaphor for spiritual illumination, and green vistas and gardens as indicators of spiritual growth and life. Greenery and light are two things Bahá'u'lláh loved dearly and was deprived of for much of the time He was a prisoner and exile over a period of forty years.

In spite of that deprivation, one landmark in His ministry—His declaration as a Manifestation of God—transpired in a garden in Baghdad. And today the surroundings of His shrine and that of the Báb on Mount Carmel include some of the most beautiful gardens on the planet. They were created so that any who visit the area may enjoy them and, like the diverse members of the Bahá'í Faith itself, the plants that make up these stunning sanctuaries come from every part of the earth. There are even trees and plants right in the center of Bahá'u'lláh's shrine, which, like that of the Báb, is flooded with light.

In the golden glow of the Báb's shrine a feeling of spiritual reunion touched me in a sweetly unexpected way. It was close to sunset on the eve of the Jewish Sabbath, when many in the Haifa area close their shops or leave work early to prepare for it. A mood of impending reverence and quiet settled in as the streets grew vacant.

As I sat quietly in the shrine in prayer and reflection, aware of the atmosphere of spiritual preparation going on all over the city, I suddenly heard the tolling of bells from the Carmelite monastery located near one of the caves of the Old Testament prophet Elijah. More lovers of God turning to prayer as the day drew to a close.

Then, from the minaret of a nearby mosque, the melodious call to prayer began to sound with soul-stirring beauty.

And we Bahá'ís, assembled from throughout the world, lovers of all faiths, with personal roots in many different ones, were gathered in the spot that honors One Whose martyrdom, akin to Christ's, aimed to free mankind from its deepest bondage and help it come together in love and unity.

As human beings grow, they lead the most spiritually actualized lives not when they cling to the familiar, but when they learn to embrace ever-widening circles and bonds with others. The pain in the world today seems directly proportionate to the degree to which we haven't yet found the love for God and each other that will transcend ourselves and will make us eager to seek God, by whatever name we call Him, in every face we see. As Bahá'u'lláh said, "the changeless Faith of God, eternal in the past, eternal in the future,"[5] draws a circle meant to include each and every one of us.

CHAPTER 6

THE LIGHT OF JUSTICE

*"The light of men is Justice. Quench it not with the contrary
winds of oppression and tyranny. The purpose of justice
is the appearance of unity among men."*

—Bahá'u'lláh, *Tablets of Bahá'u'lláh*

For Whom the Bell Did Not Toll

*Thirst for true liberty and spiritual freedom inspired one woman's
journey out of slavery in America's most famous household.*

I wonder how Ona Judge, once a slave in the home of George
Washington, celebrated the Fourth of July, or whether she observed
the holiday at all?

Though she spent the greater part of her life in my home state of
New Hampshire, she had lived literally in the shadow of the Liberty
Bell in Philadelphia—without a taste of the freedom it has come
to represent. Born into slavery in the home of Martha Washington,
her story reflects the lengths to which the human soul will go in its
yearning for true freedom.

The Liberty Bell itself has a history full of irony. When it first
arrived from where it had been cast in London and was hung outside
the Pennsylvania State House to test its sound, it cracked at the stroke
of its own clapper, a rather inauspicious sign. Tradition maintains
that it was tolled in 1774 to declare the inauguration of the first
Continental Congress, but historians don't always agree about this.
It was abolitionist newspaperman William Lloyd Garrison who first
coined the name "Liberty Bell" to describe it when it was used as a
symbol of freedom in a pamphlet produced in 1839 by the American
Anti-Slavery Society.

Although the bell was recast after it cracked, a second crack occurred
that required it to be repaired yet again in 1846. Perhaps days later,
the bell was rung for several hours in honor of George Washington's
birthday. It was during that time that a crack advanced from the top of
the repaired crack to the crown, rendering the bell unusable.

A venerable part of the nation's history all the same, the bell was
removed from its tower in 1852 and displayed to the public in a
variety of locations, the most recent, and presumably final, the
Liberty Bell Center pavilion in Philadelphia, just south of where
George Washington lived in the 1790s. At that time, this home was
the equivalent of the White House, which had yet to be built in what
was then the wilderness of the future District of Columbia.

Now some have argued, perhaps with tongue firmly in cheek, that the bell was a lemon from the start, or a bit of mischief on the part of the British foundry that cast it. But if you look at the history of the bell, and of the life of one woman who lived about five feet from where it stood, you find an interesting interplay between the words with which we often speak of liberty and the actions that have resulted in its denial to so many.

During the recent design and construction of the bell's display pavilion, planners discovered that the site was adjacent to the living quarters of black people who had been enslaved—that is, owned by the "Father of Our Country." Some accounts then go on to describe the "decision" to acknowledge this fact and the "debate" that this led to.

Debate about what, I had to ask myself. It is a fact that the first president of a nation founded on liberty and justice for all—and built on an economy of enslaving others—was a slaveholder. His wife, Martha, was an even more affluent slaveholder. What was to debate or decide? Whether this historic site, currently administered by the National Park Service, was going to acknowledge this truth?

It was becoming increasingly difficult to hide or deny this part of our Founding Father's story as archaeologists at the neighboring site of Washington's house were unearthing it room by room. And, it turned out, visitors to the Liberty Bell were accessing the bell by walking directly over the quarters where the home's slaves had been housed.

Among those enslaved servants was Ona Judge, hopefully a figure who will one day have name recognition for every American school child well beyond the prodigious hilltops of New Hampshire. Hers is a tale of how a black woman challenged and bested her "master," who also happened to be the leader of the nation.

"Born into" the slave-holdings of Martha Washington, Ona had become a famous face herself, one often seen at the many grand events Martha hosted, and which Ona's arduous workdays made possible. At the age of fifteen Ona had already had one wrenching parting from all of those she knew and loved when she was one of seven slaves to leave Mount Vernon and accompany the First Family to its new Philadelphia executive residence.

Small surprise that when Martha announced her intention a few years later to bestow Ona as a wedding gift upon her granddaughter, Ona, whose trustworthiness and good service facilitated her coming and going freely in Philadelphia, simply walked out the front door while the family was eating dinner. Uneventful as it was, this escape would have brought severe penalties had she been caught.

Heaven knows what pluck and resourcefulness helped her get all the way to Portsmouth, New Hampshire, where she was promptly recognized on the street by the daughter of Senator John Langdon, as the Langdons knew the Washingtons very well. Ironically, although in covert ways, it would be Langdon who would help Ona keep her freedom by ensuring she had sufficient warning whenever Washington's appointed agents came to find her.

Ona made a life for herself as a free black, even as she knew that slave-hunters could appear at any time to seize her, along with any children she might have, and she'd have no recourse at all. "Mistress of her needle," as Washington himself had called her, she found work as a seamstress and married a black sailor, Jack Staines, and the couple had three children.

Some years later, after his retirement from the presidency, Washington—no doubt at the chiding insistence of an outraged Martha, said to be the stronger personality of the two—dispatched yet another hunter, his nephew Burwell Bassett, Jr., to try to fetch Ona back. Once again John Langdon's intervention helped warn her in advance.

Although Ona died a ward of the state in her own home in 1848, having outlived her children, the citizens in her small community of Greenland, New Hampshire, cared about her enough to help keep her stocked with essentials. Her life as a free woman was unquestionably more difficult, in terms of material comforts, than it would have been had she stayed with the Washingtons. More than once she was asked how she could relinquish the "silks and satins" of that "fine way of life" she had known for inevitable poverty. Her reply: "I am free, and have, I trust, been made a child of God by the means."[1]

It seems it was richness in spirit Ona was after, perhaps having already understood that while her former master and mistress had been surrounded by material wealth, they hadn't necessarily been the happier for it. Ona knew what that Liberty Bell had come to symbolize, knew where true wealth and freedom lay: in the ability to read and learn; to worship as she chose; and to spend her time as she, herself, determined to.

In the Hidden Words, Bahá'u'lláh wrote:

O Son of My Handmaid! Be not troubled in poverty nor confident in riches, for poverty is followed by riches, and riches are followed by poverty. Yet to be poor in all save God is a wondrous gift, belittle not the value thereof, for in the end it will make thee rich in God, and thus thou shalt know the meaning of the utterance, "In truth ye are the poor," and the holy words, "God is the all-possessing," shall even as the true morn break forth gloriously resplendent upon the horizon of the lover's heart, and abide secure on the throne of wealth.[2]

Ona surely understood this kind of real security. I wonder how history will come to view and redefine the kind of liberty that's been symbolized by a bell that lost its voice, and by a woman who found hers and sounded the bell of her own freedom.

Some Things Call for Intolerance

At what point might our values determine that freedom of speech was never intended as license to debase others—and ourselves?

The topic of the use—and misuse—of the power of speech has certainly had its hour in the spotlight in recent years. It's interesting to note the reactive response that offensive public utterance can elicit and to wonder just when and how we'll be willing to dig down and address the roots of it all. At what point might our values determine that freedom of speech was never intended as license to debase others—and ourselves?

When a friend of mine recently chaperoned a school field trip, she was appalled at the way the kids spoke to and treated each other. As the bus lurched along, Mary was treated to an earful of what the driver overhears daily—merciless teasing as grade-school peers freely branded each other with an assortment of rude names. She also got to watch her own children, whom she knows as kind and considerate people, scanning uncomfortably between her and their schoolmates.

At home, her children know that teasing and name-calling aren't just discouraged, they're *unacceptable*. Mary and her husband aren't unrealistic enough to believe that they can keep their children from sibling battles, but they stringently enforce a standard requiring that all members of their family speak to each other with respect, even in the midst of disagreements. If emotions run too high, then each needs to take time out until civility can be restored.

"They know how serious we are about this because my husband and I hold ourselves to the same high standard of civil behavior and consideration of others' feelings," Mary says.

On the bus that day she finally spoke up in a forceful voice that knows how to get attention quickly: "The teasing and rudeness stop right here or the field trip does, and we go back and sit in school for the rest of the day. Everybody understand?"

They did, and after a period of uncomfortable silence, quiet conversations eventually resumed until the young riders reached their destination.

Like a number of other adults I know, Mary has grown impatient with a somewhat pervasive attitude that kids are naturally mean to each other and that, as long as things don't escalate into physical violence, that's the most we can hope for. Teasing and other verbal and emotional abuse are accepted as givens, as if it were inevitable for children to be nasty and even downright cruel to one another. While political correctness tries to quash racial or sexual taunts, when it comes to garden-variety insults, anything goes.

"Not in my house, and not within my hearing anywhere else, either," Mary says firmly. "I simply tell them that that's enough. Unlike the old adage about sticks and stones, names and teasing *do* hurt and are usually even more damaging and long-lasting."

Tolerance is a common theme that adults use when trying to address and discourage bullying and teasing. But how about a little *intolerance* for such hateful behavior, she suggests, giving an unmistakable message that says, "You are behaving in an unacceptable way, and we're not going to tolerate it."

There's one childhood memory that still guides my conscience and has helped police my behavior for decades now. My best friend's father was one of my favorite people in the world. He was the quintessential great dad—kind, soft-spoken, gently humorous, and thoughtful. A hard-working man with a big family, he always made time to interact with his kids and their friends, whether drawing caricatures of us as we watched, giggling all the while, or hunkering down his six-foot-six-inch frame to help us construct the miniature villages that took over his living-room floor.

Whenever he spoke with me, as he always made time to do, I felt supremely special, as though I truly mattered. Their family had a household standard about respectful behavior among all members that was similar to that of my chaperoning friend.

One day this kind dad gave me a real gift, even though it felt like something quite different at the time. I was riding in the backseat of his wood-paneled station wagon after he'd picked up a small gang of us from a Girl-Scout Christmas party. We were all comparing the gifts we'd drawn in the gift exchange, and I wasn't very happy with mine. When one of my peers leaned over and observed under her breath that someone had obviously spent the low end of the price range for it, I felt license to begin holding forth on how worthless and disappointing it was and how unfair that I had received it. I was probably enjoying my companions' attention as I bewailed my plight and began berating both the gift and the giver.

I'll never forget the look in that dad's eyes as they met mine in the rearview mirror and he said evenly but firmly, "Hey now, that's *enough*." I'd never heard this man raise his voice, and he didn't this time—just set an unambiguous limit. Although I wanted to leap from the car or otherwise disappear at that moment, I've been as grateful to him for this unexpected disciplinary action as I have for the hundreds of kindnesses he bestowed on me.

Knowing that he was disappointed and displeased with my behavior had an enormous impact on me. I was stunned and then, appropriately, embarrassed and remorseful.

He didn't need to point out how potentially hurtful what I was saying was or that the donor of that gift could have been sitting in the car, for all I knew. Awareness of all of this came to me very quickly once I was jolted out of my little rant.

All he had to tell me, this man whose opinion I cared about so much, was that it was time to stop, with four words that changed my life forever. He spoke up when my behavior was eroding into meanness and helped set a limit for me that has somehow become internally reinforcing. I believe he helped activate a healthy sense of shame, and I'm eternally grateful.

Regarding the power of what we say, Bahá'u'lláh wrote, "Every word is endowed with a spirit, therefore the speaker or expounder should carefully deliver his words at the appropriate time and place, for the impression which each word maketh is clearly evident and perceptible. The Great Being saith: One word may be likened unto fire, another unto light, and the influence which both exert is manifest in the world."[3]

As the years go by, it becomes more important than ever to me to be mindful about what I say, to ask for divine assistance in guarding my tongue so that my words will be only of benefit, never of harm. Yet sometimes when we encounter hurtful speech around us, just like my friend and that dad who helped me head off my own unpleasant behavior, it's simply time to say enough is enough.

Not Nearly Enough

*Sometimes the very ignorance behind injustice can
actually be the agent that helps to rectify it.*

It's a mission of mine to gather the stories of those who personally
experienced the demoralizing—and often dangerous—effects of
racial segregation in America, as well as the tumultuous process of
desegregation that sought to correct it.

I want to do this because the stories have been given so little
attention, and I fear that they may be lost if we don't gather them
soon. Also, I'm hoping that if they are shared creatively, especially
with younger readers and listeners, they'll provide a different window
into a piece of our history, one that looks into the personal lives of
those who experienced these painful and trying moments.

I also consider these stories significant because the actions of those
within them often exemplify the very qualities and traits we need as a
nation to overcome a legacy of unconscious superiority and suspicion
that, fueled by blind imitation and fear, still keeps us so separate. My
guess is that until we get this long-standing imbalance right, the rest
of our mounting problems, both at home and in the wider world,
won't go away.

The idea to collect these was born during an African-American
History Month event when I sat next to a friend who, as the keynote
speaker remarked on the progress made in America's race relations,
said quietly under her breath, "But not enough. Not nearly enough."
She's a community-minded person who's well liked and respected,
and she isn't one to complain. But in those quiet undertones, I could
hear her disappointment and pain as a black woman.

The stories I've been gathering are often simple ones—a seventeen-
year-old's first brave trip to the only lunch counter in his tiny town;
a young woman's difficult days as the first black student in a newly
integrated school; a white businessman confronting an angry mob
in the doorway of the home of his African-American friends where
he had arrived for a visit—but they show in everyday ways the
courage and moral conviction of blacks and whites alike who stood

up to something that was clearly wrong, no matter what the mass of those around them did or didn't do. They were everyday heroes who sacrificed their personal comfort or safety, or even risked their lives, to stand by what was right in the face of seemingly unyielding ignorance, indifference, and injustice.

What has surprised me about such stories is that, while they evoke lots of feelings, which is part of what can make them so effective in healing a divide we often have trouble acknowledging, those feelings aren't always about anger, hurt, or sadness. One story reminded me that sometimes the very ignorance behind injustice can actually be the agent that helps to rectify it.

A man described a time when he was traveling home on leave to Indiana after basic training at a military base in the South. Weeks later he would ship out with many other black Americans to boost the struggling U.S. forces in Korea. But on this day, dressed in his stiff khakis, he was waiting at a bus depot in the Deep South. It was a day of three-digit temperatures before noon, and the starched collar of his uniform was tight on his neck. As he entered the depot, he looked longingly at the air-conditioned waiting room to one side.

But instead he turned toward the cramped, stifling room marked "Colored" and ordered a cheeseburger at its small counter. His family, like many African-American families, showed a wide variety of skin colors owing to a heritage of African, Native American, and European ancestry. The options that this gave the light-skinned man were quickly brought to his attention when the man behind the counter leaned over to talk with him.

After some cordial chat, the older man lowered his voice and told the young soldier, "Now look, there's no reason for you to get that nice uniform all mussed in here where it's too hot to breathe. You're serving your country, you deserve a break. Nobody here's gonna know the difference if you go over there with the white folks and have your lunch where it's cool."

The room grew quiet as the young soldier thanked the man, then told him that he was happy to stay where he was. If others could put up with the discomfort, then he could, too. His reply drew warm smiles and nods from around the room.

He'd just taken the first few bites of his lunch when two white police officers strode in. The room fell silent as the two made their way toward him. As he braced himself for whatever was coming, he was surprised by the conciliatory tone of the officer who did all the talking.

"Son," the officer said, "you've obviously made a mistake. We know you're probably not familiar with the way we do things around here. But there's no reason for you to stay where you don't belong. You just take your lunch and come on over next door where you can be comfortable."

When the soldier began to explain, the man behind the counter gave him a warning look and the police officer said, "Now, we sure don't want any trouble. You'd best come with us and be with your *own* kind." His tone had grown firm.

There was another moment or two of silence, and then, in the face of such insistence, the soldier shrugged and rose to comply. One officer stooped to heft up the young soldier's duffle bag while the other policeman carried his plate and glass of milk carefully. Every single pair of eyes in the room watched as the two accompanied the young soldier deferentially, as if escorting a visiting dignitary.

The most memorable moment came after the room's double doors closed behind the three men and, after a beat of silence, the entire room broke into a chorus of delighted cheers and applause. The soldier, now a grandfather, says he figures that a whole lot of his ancestors must have been cheering right along with them.

Why I'm Not a Party Girl

*The Bahá'í Faith's approach to the democratic process leaves
no room for partisanship and increases the likelihood that
those elected will truly work for the well-being of all.*

This week, my town, my whole state has an aura of calm after the storm.

The weather has something to do with that. After relentless weeks of deep freeze and deep snow that has arrived in wave after wave over this last month, we're finally having a thaw. It's possible to walk safely on most surfaces again, and far safer at intersections, where you can now actually see around the corner as the mountainous snow banks shrink.

Probably one of the nicest days we've had so far this winter worked to the advantage of the other kind of whirlwind that engulfed our state recently, the one in which folks lined up in record numbers to cast their vote in New Hampshire's now nationally famous presidential primary.

Along with the change in the weather, there was another sort of calm after the storm last Wednesday morning here in New Hampshire. We finally had our phones and our streets back. The day before the election, I had counted six calls in four minutes, four of which proceeded to leave a prerecorded political message on our answering machine. Then not one, but three separate visitors came to my door to ask whether I had been downtown to cast my vote.

While politics was the inevitable topic du jour wherever one went these last weeks, I wasn't one of those campaigning on the corner for my favorite candidate. It's not because I don't care about public policy or because I don't prize my right to vote. Lord knows too many people sacrificed too much to give all of us the opportunity to do so, and I don't take this privilege—and civic duty—lightly. I've volunteered in voter-registration campaigns and offered transportation to polling places. I'm very committed to exercising my vote and encouraging others to do so.

And, without a doubt, I'm heartened by the response to the current state of affairs that I see among increasing numbers of people, especially those under the age of thirty. They are asking good questions, sometimes large and possibly unsettling ones, and they are taking a deep and personal interest in public policy. They are manifesting Bahá'u'lláh's admonition to "Be anxiously concerned with the needs of the age ye live in, and center your deliberations on its exigencies and requirements."[4]

However, I cannot help but notice that so many of the messages in this political season, and in most others in previous years, are deeply divisive. Each candidate traveled up and down my state saying, in a hundred different ways, "Vote for me! Vote for me!" The partisan political process seems to foster personal ambition, disunity, distressing public discourse, vapid slogans, and the struggle for power.

There seems to be a reaction to partisanship that is surfacing in this country. Large numbers seem to have realized that the current hyper-partisan political environment has left government in a broken condition, not truly meeting the needs of the people.

People are expressing a profound hope that a new nonpartisan spirit will emerge this year. The new mantra of this political season is "change," and there's been a lot of use of the word "hope" here in New Hampshire over the past week. What remains to be seen is the perennial question of every political season: Will our elected leaders deliver on their promises? Unfortunately, in our partisan political world, all too often the results are profoundly disappointing.

By contrast, as a Bahá'í, I find something in the teachings of Bahá'u'lláh that gives me a lot of hope. The Bahá'í Faith has a very interesting electoral process of its own. The religion has no clergy, and the affairs of the community are administered through nine-member governing councils on the local, national, and international levels that are elected without any campaigning, nominations, or electioneering.

In the Bahá'í Faith, elections are sacred events, clothed in prayer, nurtured in reflection, conducted in quiet. In the absence of campaigning, the elections go forward without anyone going around saying "vote for me, vote for me!" These elections are carried out by a most egalitarian "body politic." There are no opposing candidates to sling mud at because there are no candidates at all—those who can vote are also eligible to be elected. The individual votes for those he or she thinks are best suited for service on a Bahá'í elected body.

Bahá'í elections aim to identify servants of the community who, through their own growth and maturation, particularly spiritual maturation, have acquired the kinds of attitudes, abilities, and qualities that can promote justice, dispel oppression, and foster a deep and real unity between a diverse group of people.

And being elected is not so much an opportunity to govern as it is to serve. It is a sacred duty, literally a calling from the community to arise to serve, because you didn't seek it out, and it often involves sacrifice. Having ambitions to acquire a position or striving to gain an advantage over others are the very antithesis of Bahá'í elections. Instead, leadership is expressed through humility, love for the community, and the desire to help everyone use their talents to the best of their ability.

The Faith's approach to the democratic process leaves no room for partisanship and thus increases the likelihood that those elected will not be driven by personal ambition or be bound by narrow interests, but rather will work for the well-being of all, as well as for the well-being of the entire planet.

Of course, no Bahá'í would ever claim to live up to these ideals perfectly, but in the thirty years I've been privileged to experience the Bahá'í election process, I've seen its real viability as a model of governance truly of the people, by the people, and for the people.

CHAPTER 7

GEMS OF INESTIMABLE VALUE

"The Great Being saith: Regard man as a mine rich in gems of inestimable value. Education can, alone, cause it to reveal its treasures, and enable mankind to benefit therefrom."

—Bahá'u'lláh, *Gleanings from the Writings of Bahá'u'lláh*

Baked with Loving Hands

*The very aspects of my children's natures that differ most,
the ones that once sparked battles, are among the
best things they have to offer each other today.*

It's a revealing experience to have our two grown children back in the house at the same time, even if only for the holidays.

At nineteen our daughter ventured into the wide world to teach English to kindergartners in China. She's now a Montessori school teacher and so self-disciplined and focused that she can't help but have a galvanizing effect on us. After all, she's accustomed to motivating and overseeing dozens of small children. Her balky family members are a snap by comparison.

Her brother, however, remains so laid back that we periodically feel tempted to check for a pulse. It seems to be the grand design that families frequently encompass the most unlikely groupings of folks, who often ask themselves, "What am *I* doing with these people?"

The assortment of very different individuals that typically comprise most families is a wise and divine design. Because we are so very different, we represent a pool of diversified experience and varied perspectives that is superb preparation for dealing with the world. But that's only if we're willing to receive these as the gifts they truly are. So often, those traits that differ from our own can look like things we might be tempted to call "weird," "mystifying," or even downright "annoying."

As I've watched our grown children interact, I've noticed two gratifying things. The first—balm to my mother's heart—is how much they've come to love and accept each other. The other is how much those very aspects of their natures that differ most, the ones that once sparked battles, are among the best things they have to offer each other today.

This brings to mind something that happened years ago, which I now realize was an indicator of the importance of receiving what others have to offer, especially when it seems very different from what we think we want.

When our son was nine he proudly announced that he was going to bake his sister's birthday cake. His "cooking" experience at the time consisted of peanut-butter sandwiches and microwave popcorn. Frankly, we were speechless that the idea would even occur to him. He was insistent, however, that this first baking effort, his birthday gift to her, was something he wanted to do entirely by himself.

Eager to encourage his interest in cooking, I was nevertheless concerned about how he would accomplish this while accommodating the demands of his sister's VERY particular tastes. She had big plans for how her birthday would be celebrated with sixth-grade classmates that year, and she was quite specific about exactly what kind of cake she wished to have. Having him bake it wasn't part of the plan. Fortunately, her cake of choice was available as a boxed mix, one that included brightly colored candy sprinkles.

The night before her birthday, our son plowed through his homework and then began assembling bowls and utensils. As if to reassure me, he sat down and read the package's instructions until I was sure he had them memorized and told me, "You don't need to help me. I'll just follow the instructions."

In a game of parental stealth, I tried to monitor his activities without appearing to hover, finding a dozen reasons to rummage in the kitchen.

Face contorted with concentration, he broke eggs into a bowl for the first time, measured out ingredients as though handling priceless objects, and, to my astonishment, made virtually no mess at all.

When it came time to use the electric mixer, he granted me permission only to check that all the pieces were connected properly, then thanked and dismissed me as the beaters began to whir, mixing the rich, golden batter. He had only to add the sprinkles, and the aroma of baking cake would soon fill the house.

Encouraged by his progress, I went to answer the phone and was horrified to return a few minutes later and find him wrist-deep in cake batter, working his hands in the bowl. When he saw my face, he immediately explained that he'd washed his hands VERY thoroughly before taking this highly unusual step. Then he gestured with his head toward the empty sprinkles packet on the counter beside him and said knowingly, as though the two of us shared some greater wisdom about this but sometimes you just have to go along with what you're told: "Can you BELIEVE it? It seems silly, but that's what the directions said. 'Add sprinkles and mix by HAND'!"

As I collected myself and explained the role of spoons in this process, I had to agree with him that it might have been helpful for the instructions to actually mention them.

That cake—which turned out beautifully—tasted even better for the laughter that followed as we waited for it to bake, and every time we've told the story since. What that cake showed his sister was that her brother had unexpected depths and deep affection that he wanted to share with her by giving her a special gift on her birthday. My daughter was able to help him identify a motive and focus by telling him exactly what kind of cake she wanted and, curiously, although it's on far more life-changing levels, this is exactly the kind of exchange they're still sharing today.

Since then, my son has become a cook who still likes to show his generosity by feeding others. He's also learned how to approach at least some of life's instructions with a grain or two of salt, along with all the other ingredients.

Trustworthiness: Express Lane to Honesty

Just as any physical structure needs a foundation, so a life of
any spiritual substance must be founded on truthfulness.

One day at work, I discovered that my only available exit from a room would take me smack through the middle of a conversation taking place between a teenage boy and my boss.

Their exchange appeared to be one that each would prefer to keep private. The boy looked pale and nervous. My boss seemed stiff and guarded, although obviously listening carefully. I knew I couldn't just walk through the middle of that.

The previous summer, this same boy had attended a program at the conference center where I worked and his behavior had been quite problematic. My boss, a kind man who already had too much on his plate, probably wondered what he was going to encounter with this young man now.

Although I didn't want to eavesdrop, snippets of their conversation floated my way—phrases like "really sorry" and "want to make up for it." I noticed that the teenager was doing most of the talking. When I peeked over toward them again, I could see that the boy's face looked relieved. My boss's posture had also relaxed considerably, and they finally moved away from the door so I could exit without having to interrupt them.

When I saw my boss put his hand gently on the boy's shoulder, I knew I'd witnessed one of those quietly monumental things that happen in the smallest of moments. This boy had made good on the toughest part of trustworthiness—owning up and taking responsibility for his actions. Then he'd also taken the step many never quite find the courage for: making amends.

Such trustworthiness often blossoms out of truthfulness, which Bahá'u'lláh identifies as "the foundation of all human virtues."[1] Just as any physical structure needs a foundation, so a life of spiritual substance must be founded on truthfulness.

I heard someone suggest recently that the act of acknowledging the truth about our actions and looking to set things right isn't simply to make us feel better or to relieve us of guilt or shame. The purpose is for us to learn the lessons implied in the error so that we may truly be of some good in the world.

However, to have the capacity to learn such lessons, we need training that helps us understand and appreciate their value, and we need to see this kind of behavior modeled for us in action. The very rarity of such trustworthiness in our culture today would imply that there's a considerable need for the sort of training that can help us develop the qualities of trustworthiness and truthfulness from an early age.

However, one friend's story reflects that even as adults we can experience deep epiphanies about the power of sincere amends. One woman I greatly admire had the kind of tough childhood that keeps your mind awake at night after even a brief account of it. While I know that adversity often molds us into good people, I wondered how she'd survived at all, let alone flourished as a human being.

"Oh, I have my mother to thank," she told me.

I knew that her mother's behavior had been a large part of what had made her family life so miserable. I also knew that my friend had reacted in her teens by withdrawing, having serious trouble with drug use, and making more than a few other bad choices. I'd have assumed that she was being sarcastic, but I knew sarcasm wasn't her style. She knows, and has learned through experience, that it's far too destructive.

"Years later, my mother came to me, told me there was nothing she could do to make up for what she'd done, but that she was sincerely sorry and would do anything she could to help me now," my friend said. "She meant it, and the relationship we have today compared to what I knew growing up is like a wonderful dream. I couldn't believe what a powerful and freeing thing it was for me to have someone, especially my mother, simply acknowledge the truth."

It turned out that my friend's mother had a misdiagnosed illness and the medication prescribed for her over many years had contributed to her aggressive and abusive behavior. Her mother, obviously, had felt just as miserable as the rest of her family.

"But she never once used that to justify things," my friend said. "Instead, she owned up to what she knew was wrong, gave me the gift of that, and, as a result, I now know that I can't do any less than that in my own life, no matter how justifiable anyone else might find my excuses."

The results of this, she says, have touched and benefited countless other people in both of their lives.

As that teenage boy and my boss walked away together companionably, the boy's action and my boss's response to it radiated around them so perceptibly I could feel it. I now realize that what my friend said is true. The honesty in this interaction, and the young man's ability to acknowledge and attempt to make amends for his past mistakes, will affect their lives for years to come.

When Opportunity Calls

Children's imperfect delivery often masks their very best intentions.

I've fallen in love with three-year-olds—whole rooms full of them. If you'd told me when I was a young mother that I'd one day seek out this opportunity, let alone enjoy it, I'd have thought you were crazy.

Yet now I can't seem to resist the pure, guileless beauty of children's nature at this age. They seem to reflect so much about human possibility that's so very encouraging.

Their clear-eyed—if simplified—view of the world, and the depth of inner understanding they often demonstrate, are complemented by another inborn quality, one that could really help our troubled world if we were to let ourselves be instructed and humbled by it, even a little.

Children, especially at this age, have an innate desire to help and serve. This is most often expressed as a completely openhanded offering, with no personal agenda. Unfortunately, their delivery can sometimes be a little sloppy, making it very easy to miss their intention.

As a platter of cut fruit was being passed around by a teacher during snack time in one classroom of young friends recently, everyone was doing a good job of following the rules designed to maintain order. All had their bottoms on their chairs, touched only those pieces to which they served themselves, and ate their snack quietly.

Suddenly, one child grabbed the platter and leapt to his feet. As the teacher moved to admonish him to sit down and put the platter back, she quickly recognized that his intention, even before serving himself, was to bring it to me, a guest sitting unobtrusively on the sidelines, so that I could have some snack, too. Thankfully, this spontaneous act of consideration and generosity was rewarded with praise rather than rebuffed through misunderstanding. Being able to recognize the positive intent of such actions seems an essential part of fostering them.

Sometimes when we're out of our element in unfamiliar surroundings, we can notice certain things more acutely than we usually do. This happened to me one afternoon during a semester when I was teaching English to kindergartners in China a few years back. En route by taxi to a city school, I was suddenly hit by illness that made me feel weak, shaky, and dizzy. I arrived at the school and managed to pay the driver and make my way inside but had no idea how I'd get through the afternoon of classes ahead of me.

I was greeted at the classroom door by a five-year-old boy who, upon seeing me, took my bags and carried them to a place where he pointed for me to sit. Then he disappeared into the next room and returned with water in a beautiful clay teacup. He presented this to me with marked kindness, good manners, and concern, and then stood beside me companionably, patting my back gently a few times as I sipped slowly.

He spoke only a few English words he'd learned from me (none of which applied very much in this situation) and I spoke virtually no Chinese, but the unspoken communication between us in those moments was unmistakably deep.

The only way I can describe what happened next is that I felt flooded with a warmth that actually made me feel stronger, as though my symptoms had disappeared. I also experienced a surge of energy that lifted and carried me through that class and those that followed. I feel that same warm strength every time I remember his kindness.

This boy, whose classmates were all napping when I arrived, was what his classroom teacher probably viewed as a "problem." When she discovered him with me, she immediately raised her voice to berate him but I managed to communicate that what he had done was helpful and good. I know that he, at least, understood my appreciation. His tremendous sensitivity and kindness, which had also mysteriously provided such assistance to me, could have easily been misunderstood or trampled under angry scolding.

This sweet boy's response to my need, and his teacher's misunderstanding of his kind intentions, reminded me of something that had happened with my son years ago. When my young son and I were home alone one day, he did a startling thing. For a while when he was young he was basically terrified of the telephone—even loving grandparents couldn't coax him to use it. I felt pretty nervous about the phone myself that day as I awaited a call from the editor of a national magazine, unsure as to what kind of news he'd give me about a story I was trying to sell.

As I fixed dinner, I listened for the phone and then, in disbelief, watched as my son raced toward it when it rang. Still stunned, I saw him pick up the receiver and say cheerily, "Hang up, will ya?" then do exactly that.

Our eyes met in frozen silence before it rang again. I'll never forget that look in his eyes as he slunk away to the table, where I told him to wait for me.

Fortunately, the caller not only called back and gave me happy news about my submission, but also joked that since he'd hung up my manuscript for such a long time before giving me an answer, my son's response had probably been kind of appropriate.

I immediately wanted to call four friends to share my good news, but thank heaven I first turned back to the far more important business awaiting me at the kitchen table, where my son sat looking miserable. I joined him and asked, more gently than I might have minutes before, why he'd done what he had.

"I wanted to help because you were busy," he told me as his face dissolved in tears.

With time and distance from the myopia of young motherhood, I recognize today that his intuition and sensitivity had certainly picked up on my own nervousness that day and, more than anything, he had truly wanted to help. Of course, once he'd actually pushed himself to approach the phone, his skills had been fairly limited and, from his small perspective, his first brave attempt to use it appeared to have failed dismally.

My suggested exercise of writing an "I'm sorry" note (which drew a very kind reply postcard from the friendly editor) was an attempt to help him learn some relevant life skills. But I think the most important thing I did that afternoon, the one that resonates the most more than twenty years later, was to tell him that I appreciated that he'd been trying to help me and that I was sorry that I had misunderstood.

No matter how many studies they do, researchers seem to keep coming around to the same sort of equation about human behavior: We get out of our children not only what we invest in them when raising them, but also what we accept, acknowledge, and welcome from them. There are a whole lot of young helpers out there, potentially powerful human resources for the future, just waiting for us to recognize in them the little things they're trying to offer us every day.

The Invitation in Forgiveness

*While forgiveness often comes hard for many reasons, it can be
an invitation to a new and nearly overwhelming freedom.*

Wherever I go this week, I encounter the topic of forgiveness. It's
come up in personal conversations and group discussions, in reading,
in movies, seemingly everywhere I turn.

And it's been kindled most deeply by a process that's become part
of everyday life for me these days—sorting through boxes and boxes
of my parents' belongings, now that they've both gone on to whatever
world comes after this one.

For a while, I simply couldn't get to this activity. I moved the boxes
into my home, where they accumulated steadily, forgotten in other
rooms, most of them safely out of sight. Finally, when a new batch
arrived and there was nowhere left to put them, I knew it was time
to begin.

Who knew what doors this would open? It's been like falling into
whole other worlds. There is information about my parents' lives that
is surfacing for the first time, and there's been an endless stirring of
memories, which lead to a cascade of all kinds of feelings.

Inevitably, there are also the echoes of old hurts, things it would
be easier not to remember. That, I am discovering, is an invitation to
the humbling, nearly overwhelming freedom that forgiveness offers.

One author, Erik Blumenthal, has been a valued companion on
my spiritual journey through the years ever since something I read
in one of his books knocked me right off the couch where I lay
reading. All these years later, I can still remember the words on the
page in front of me, which suggested that the person who comes to
understand his parents can *forgive* the world. I went back and read
that over again several times as I tried to grasp the very concept.

The author, who grew up Jewish in Nazi Germany, certainly knew
a thing or two about pain, injustice, and the kinds of deprivation and
suffering that can make forgiveness come very hard. Yet in his work
as a psychologist and writer, he always drew attention to the two
tasks he saw facing all human beings: to become more conscious and

more spiritual. And forgiveness is an unavoidable component of that spirituality, he asserted.

As I unpack my parents' things, I'm continually offered a larger, wider perspective that can help me see their lives whole, view them in the context of what they faced, the best efforts and decisions that they were able to make. I see two *young* (i.e., my grown children's age) people coming into a relationship in a time when no one knew what the next day would bring, who would live or die, or even what language everyone would be speaking depending on the outcome of the war still known as "The Big One." The stories my parents told, often only a fractional glimpse of something so much larger, take on a whole new meaning for me now. And whatever challenges I face that can keep me from forgiving past wrongdoings seem to soften and fade.

It's as though I'm watching movie-like vignettes of two people who, whatever their circumstances, troubles, and often significant mistakes or missteps, nonetheless made a place for me in this world and stuck with that commitment. As so many new little pieces of a bigger story come together, I'm reminded of a phrase from Rúmí so essential as to almost be stating the obvious, yet carrying a profound truth: "When you eventually see through the veils to how things really are, you will keep saying again and again, this is certainly not like we thought it was."[2]

Forgiveness can be a tough prospect in the face of memories and experiences that are too painful for families like mine to even talk about. We had encountered within the disease of alcoholism, a great waster of lives in so many ways, the incredible barrier it posed to communication and intimacy.

Yet as I contemplate and continue to uncover a broader view of the lives my parents lived, I see that so often, my own resistance to forgiveness seems to have been forged when I was much younger, at a stage of my life when the imprint of my parents' perceived omnipotence led me to believe that they were always in charge, in the know, in control of any situation that arose. What I can share with them now, after being a parent myself for many years, is the sure knowledge that that was never true. This has led me to the humbling realization that, whatever the hurts, it is not, indeed, as I thought it was.

As I discover more about these two people who loved and cared for me in ways revealed new before me each day, I realize that we almost never know the full context of someone else's circumstances. But when we accept something about someone, including things that in the past may have seemed confusing or troubling, compassion inevitably follows. And, more often than not, we usually have to call upon greater help from beyond our own small selves to find our way toward true forgiveness and the wondrous release that it brings.

It's been observed that many may draw back from forgiveness because they believe that it might go against the grain of justice, might excuse a wrong or deny its occurrence. But when we find a willingness to try to see beyond our own view about any situation, especially when we try to understand the actions of others, it seems to take away the power that the fear holds and enables us to experience freedom from whatever hurt we are still holding inside.

CHAPTER 8

COMMIT YOUR AFFAIRS TO HIS KEEPING

"Put your trust in God, and commit your affairs to His keeping."

—Bahá'u'lláh, quoted in *The Advent of Divine Justice*

Within Calamity, Providence Awaits

We are all connected, supremely related. And there's
so much more going on than we can see.

Not long ago I received news from two different families that unimaginable tragedy had struck them both. Their stories have stayed with me, not so much because of their pain and sadness, but because of the sense of wonder each provoked, a reminder that everything that happens always has larger ramifications than what we see on the surface, and often extends further than we imagine.

A friend's daughter lost her husband in a single-car accident on a country road late at night as he was driving home from work. Their family was in the process of relocating to another state, and the husband was finishing up a few details before joining his wife and children in their new home. Then, in a heartbeat, the wife was a widow flying north for a funeral and preparing to raise three children without their father.

In the days of deep shock that followed, my friend's one focus was to help her daughter feel that her husband's presence was close by. My friend had already experienced deep grief herself, and in her strong faith she knew that believing in a loved one's presence would be a lifeline for her daughter in the days to come.

As they lived through the funeral and the anguished hours when, together, they went through the few belongings he'd kept with him after the family moved, she says that there were countless little evidences of his nearness. These felt like "small visits from him," she said, whether it was a card he'd written to his family but hadn't had time to mail, or the dozen times in those days when they couldn't figure out what to do next and the answer would just seem to appear.

When it came time to fly home, my friend's daughter was carrying some of her husband's belongings with her when she was faced with the rigorous airport security most travelers now encounter. The strain of the previous days suddenly caused her to break down, unable to take another step. She was terrified that they wouldn't allow her to board the plane with the box she clutched like her most precious possession, and she collapsed in the face of the final, greater separation that this implied.

As officials took the box from her to gently examine and verify its contents, a trio of huge men appeared, all of them security personnel, and engulfed her in an embrace, essentially catching her in their arms between them. Each, it turns out, had suffered a recent, unexpected loss—one, a wife; another, a brother; the third, a very close friend. They knew how she felt, how difficult this particular moment was for her. They came to her like family and surrounded her with their unhurried and empathetic support. It was, my friend says, exactly what her daughter's husband would have done, and it was, perhaps, his most important "visit" during the ordeal of those days.

When the daughter arrived home, she called her mother to share the story of what had happened at the airport and to say that she'd also learned something that was a big solace—that the body of her husband, long an advocate of organ donation, had benefited five people after his death.

Shortly after I heard this, we received an e-mail from my husband's sister, Happy, and I knew when the subject line was simply her husband's name that the message held potentially grave news. She's also a young mother of three, and her husband, Will, has seen some very difficult war duty in Iraq. We were all thankful when he came home; yet the prospect of his return to Iraq still loomed over his family.

The message described yet another accident that had occurred in the wee hours of the morning. Will, a paratrooper, had been at night-jump practice when another paratrooper above him had blocked out the wind to Will's parachute, causing it to collapse. As he was too close to the ground to pull his reserve chute, Will had had no choice but to get into position and prepare for landing. The lower part of his spine was crushed by the impact of the fall.

Happy received the call at about 3 a.m., around the same time that other young wife had gotten her middle-of-the-night call. Happy had been waiting for Will to get home so that they could embark on the two-week vacation their family had awaited for such a long and uncertain time. At this point, as I was reading the e-mail, I almost wondered whether I could continue.

She went on to say how thankful she is for friends who'll watch her children on a moment's notice and treat them like their own. And for the friends who unhesitatingly accompanied her to the hospital where, not knowing what was to come, she spent eleven very long hours in an intensive-care waiting room as Will underwent surgery. Although her message was necessarily abbreviated, she took a whole paragraph to express her gratitude about others' support, as though breathing it in again and remembering the comfort of it.

It turns out that, because someone who had died that day had donated his body to science, the surgeons were able to repair Will's spine. Will was going to have a long recovery, and his jumping days were over, but he was going to walk, he was going to live—and he was coming home.

"My calamity is My providence," Bahá'u'lláh has written of the way in which greater forces work within all our lives, "outwardly it is fire and vengeance, but inwardly it is light and mercy. Hasten thereunto that thou mayest become an eternal light and an immortal spirit."[1]

Now I don't honestly know whether it was the man from that first family whose body provided what Will needed. But the proximity of these two incidents and the parallels between them linger in my mind.

I hope we won't miss the rays of light—eternal light—that break through and offer the assurance that we are connected to each other, often in unexpected ways, and that there's so much more going on than we can see. One of the brightest aspects of that light, like all those people who reached out to these two young women, is what we have to offer to each other.

How to Avoid a Big Stink

What if real wisdom—and freedom—comes from knowing
what to overlook, as well as what to heed?

"The art of wisdom is the art of knowing what to overlook."

When I turned over this quote from William James on my calendar recently, it struck a chord that reverberated long afterward.

I've made several trips out of the United States in recent months, and each time I return, I bring with me two kinds of longing. One is a desire to see my home country again, as I genuinely love it, and the other is a yearning to subtract at least some degree of the "there's never enough time" mania from my life, the one that seems so much a part of the culture I live in. It is the driven, fast-paced nature of such a lifestyle that particularly confounds me. When I'm away from it, in surroundings that don't seem to reinforce a message that I'm not quite worthy if I'm not in some sort of perpetual motion, I can see it clearly for what it is. I can even begin to make plans for how I might change this overly booked, almost frantic way of life once I return home.

But when I am home, immersed in and surrounded by it, I'm truly like one of those frogs in water that's gradually coming to a boil. I can't perceive its grip or effect on me, nor understand how I get caught up in it despite my earnest efforts to avoid it.

As this pace only increases, the imperative for consciously slowing down and choosing how to respond—rather than increasing the rate at which we react—seems obvious. James's words appeared like a touchstone for me, a reminder that conscious living doesn't usually fall victim to either time or circumstance, but masters them by allowing neither to control it. However, it takes a very deliberate kind of living to move beyond the fight-or-flight reaction that's so often stimulated by the ever-increasing "urgent" messages coming our way, whether from "official information" sources or our overfull e-mail in-boxes.

As I've been assisting in a preschool class a few hours each month, my time in the company of three-year-olds has reinforced for me the validity of James's observation. There simply couldn't be adequate space or time to react to every new, emotionally charged development that comes along in a three-year-old's day. Responsible, life-experienced adults have to be selective in deciding what truly requires a meaningful response, and what it is wiser, nay, perhaps even safer to simply overlook, and instead focus on something positive or more important (which, mercifully, can be fairly easy to do with three-year-olds).

As one friend put it, in order to achieve real quality of life, we sometimes have to follow James's wisdom about NOT reacting, about letting some things go—perhaps even doing nothing. This may require riding out a considerable storm of panicked energy inside us that insists that action is required. But like anything else, not reacting becomes easier to do with conscious practice.

As if on cue, someone shared a story that was about as concrete an example of this as I could ever imagine. My neighbor had been wrestling with her cat's schedule, which involved a lot of nocturnal going in and out that was upsetting the cat-owner's sleep considerably. Finally, she decided to resolve the issue by opening the screen of her bedroom window (whose sill is quite close to the ground) to facilitate the cat's nighttime travels.

A few days later, this woman awoke one night to the sound of scratching in her bedroom—a sound that she knew right away was NOT being produced by her cat. It didn't take long to recognize the source, something in some ways similar to a cat, but which can also leave an awfully big stink in its wake.

Now, if this isn't a cause for inner alarm and subsequent reaction, I can't imagine what is. There you are in the quiet vulnerability of your own bedroom when you wake to find that you've got a skunk for company. Every terror-driven reflex I've got would be screaming for me to run for my life at that moment, which, of course, would be exactly the wrong thing to do. This woman had the admirable presence of mind to recognize that right away.

Her survival instincts took a page from animal wisdom and decided that playing possum was definitely the best available option. She steadied herself to lie quietly and began thinking how things would likely go if she didn't overreact or, in this case, react at all.

125

A skunk that had found its way in was highly likely to find its way out again, she reminded herself, and she was at least in a prime location to know when that had finally transpired. The challenge was just how much exploring it would do in the interim, whether it might fall asleep under a couch somewhere, perhaps, although the laws of basic instinct probably ensured that it would be drawn irresistibly back outside before the light of the new day.

So, this wise woman lay very quietly (although very wakefully) and listened and waited. At some point, she heard the sound of the cat's dish on the kitchen floor and eventually, thankfully, the scuffling sounds of the critter returning to her bedroom and then, the sounds of it finding its way back outside again. Phew!

This was where she was especially wise and let some more time elapse, quite a bit more time, before she got up carefully and closed that screen, which you can bet she will never leave open again.

That's the point in the story where I'd have definitely blown it, if I could even have found the will to simply lie still and let things run their course. It took wisdom and faith to recognize that the best course of action was taking almost no action at all. Reacting, however, could have easily created a really big stink to deal with later.

My guess is that my neighbor already had some practice with knowing what to overlook, when to let something run its course, or how to respond with that Zen-like deliberate choice to do nothing. On top of James's words, she left me with a fine inner metaphor to reference the next time life offers me an invitation to avoid what could potentially become a big stink, too.

Patience Brings Its Own Perks

*The ills all flesh is heir to also affect those who try to
make patience a priority, but they only touch the surface.
The depths are calm and serene.*

There was no way I could miss her. She was literally sitting on her hands, wriggling all over, feet swinging like small hammers as her gaze darted around the room. She was about five, and it was obvious she was doing everything in her power to stay in her chair at a local café.

When she finally spotted me watching her, she burst forth eagerly, "I'm being patient!"

"You sure are, and you're doing a really good job, too," I answered, sorry I hadn't thought to tell her so first. Usually, when I see children waiting with at least some degree of willingness, I say something such as "Thank you for being patient," because after fifty-plus years of effort, I know how hard it can be.

Her mother's conversation with a friend drew to a close, and they went on their way, which no doubt made that kindergartner, who had worked so hard to contain her energy and not interrupt the grown-ups, very happy.

She's an example I've thought back to as the months have gone by. I've determined that patience is something I want to give a bigger role in my life. I want to hear myself say "That's all right, I can wait" more often and really mean it, and truly *practice* patience— consciously and willingly. I want to arrive at a place where I can trust that whatever I'm waiting for will work out.

When we utilize patience to react to fewer stressors and potential irritants, eventually, many of them stop hitting our inner radar screen at all. That way, as someone far wiser than I once explained, stressors will only touch the surface of our lives. Inside, we will remain "calm and serene."

The speaker was 'Abdu'l-Bahá, who also said that "all our sorrow, pain, shame and grief, are born in the world of matter; whereas the spiritual Kingdom never causes sadness. A man living with his

127

thoughts in this Kingdom knows perpetual joy. The ills all flesh is heir to do not pass him by, but they only touch the surface of his life, the depths are calm and serene."[2]

'Abdu'l-Bahá was someone who certainly suffered greatly in his life, but he also knew supreme happiness and constantly encouraged it in others. He demonstrated how, by having that calm inner certainty, we can accept whatever the outcome in the situations before us.

"Genius is nothing but a greater aptitude for patience," Benjamin Franklin wrote, while John Quincy Adams once remarked that "Patience and perseverance have a magical effect before which difficulties disappear and obstacles vanish."

In order to be genuine, patience also seems to require a quiet trust and expectation that things will turn out right. In her small, early efforts, that young model of patience in the café was summoning these things, even though she could barely stay in her seat.

What also inspired me in her example was her attitude. She was willing to believe she could do it and to try really hard to achieve it, even if it was difficult. If I can cultivate an attitude like that, I stand half a chance of success because I know, from far too much experience, how tough things can feel when my patience feels "tried."

In addition to practicing calm acceptance in the face of difficult times, patience often means doing something now so that it will bear fruit later, like planting a seed and waiting for it to grow. In this way, especially, patience is a commitment to the future, one big reason why I want to make an extra effort at it.

Patience is not only a way of responding to something but also an approach to living in itself, one that acknowledges the principle of "right timing" in the unfolding of things.

Friends of ours suddenly found themselves without a car when theirs died, and they needed to replace it. The husband's unhurried approach to this became an object of study for me. As the weeks passed, he shopped rather thoroughly, investigating a wide variety of choices. Meanwhile, his wife, who normally does a lot of traveling and commuting, saw this as an opportunity to change her normally hectic lifestyle. "This is the first time in a LONG time that I've been able to just spend some unscheduled time at home, take my time, reading what I want to read. We'll get a car, eventually," she told me, unfazed.

In the months to come, like that little girl, I may also have to sit on my hands and even swing my legs a bit, at times, to maintain patience. But I aspire even more to be like my friend with the car-shopping husband. She was savvy enough to simply look around for something to do with the "found" time life gave her when things didn't go according to plan. That was practicing insightful wisdom as well as patience.

The Main Course

*After decades of horrific holidays at the hands of others' erratic
or downright abusive behavior, my friend Nadine hatched
a plan for the "perfect" Thanksgiving meal.*

It's amazing how deeply expectations, lying in wait, grow embedded
in us through years of holiday seasons only to reemerge again each
year when the time for celebration rolls around again.

After decades of horrific holidays at the hands of others' erratic or
downright abusive behavior, my friend Nadine hatched a plan for the
perfect Thanksgiving meal in her own home. It was her big strategy to
record new memories over the tapes of those earlier nightmares.

She planned a menu with enough side dishes, vegetables, baked
goods, appetizers, and desserts to make any table groan. Then, to top
it all off, she decided to surprise her New England guests with the
very last thing they'd ever be expecting—a genuine Southern ham.

Her mouth watered as she recalled the delicious thin slices that had
accompanied those carbohydrate-dense breakfasts she'd been served
down South. Wouldn't her guests be surprised and delighted when
she served up this special treat?

She had invited about a dozen of them and knew that she'd have
to spend some money to accommodate such a crowd. It turned out to
be a considerable investment indeed—sixty-five dollars alone for the
twenty-five pound beauty that would be the table's centerpiece.

Imagine her surprise when the ham arrived packed in a burlap sack
inside its shipping box and, on top of that, was the most remarkable
(and repugnant) shade of green. As she was about to reach for the
phone, she decided to read the accompanying instructions first. Sure
enough, this item was actually *supposed* to look this way. Part of the
curing process had involved burying the ham in the ground, and
this curious hue was the result of that earthy process and absolutely
nothing to fear, the brochure advised.

The next step would be to soak this unwieldy green slab for
several days. This proved a particular challenge, as Nadine had no
container large enough to hold the ham together with the copious

amount of water needed to cover it—other than her bathtub. So, over the next few days, she and her husband and their two teenage sons spent lots of time jockeying this heavy, slippery object between the tub and a stainless steel trash can each time one of them needed to bathe.

Once the soaking process was complete, it was time to remove that green coating, a task made significantly more difficult by the ham's now-viscous surface. Once Nadine, her husband, and their marriage had survived this excruciatingly arduous process, with all of the sharp objects it involved, most of which had to be sharpened at least twice, it was time to actually cook the ham. Nadine's giant lobster pot allowed exactly half of it to be submerged at once, so that's how she cooked it, one half at a time.

It really is a testament to her ability to hold a vision that she was still able to imagine an appetizing meal emerging out of all this, but she's not one to get discouraged easily. She had purchased fresh pineapple with the plan of anchoring slices of it to the ham with toothpicks. Unfortunately, no toothpicks could have withstood the pounding required to hammer them into this main course. She served the pineapple on the side.

By this point, the tension was really ramping up as the guests were arriving. While the other food was all coming together beautifully, the ham was still being . . . uncooperative. Nadine's husband was sharpening and resharpening knives and only half-joking as he began to talk about getting the chainsaw from the shed.

The hunks of meat that finally appeared on the guests' plates seemed equally impenetrable and, sadly, proved inedible. Whenever it was possible to actually chew a mouthful, the ham's brackish saltiness made it hard to imagine swallowing it. There was a reason, Nadine now realized, why those slices on her restaurant plate down south had been so paper-thin.

The guests feasted that day on everything but that special dish. Nadine made everyone take some of it home with them, if only to bury in the backyard.

"And to think, some poor pig had to give its life for this," she later sighed over the pumpkin pie.

That was the last "special meal" she ever pinned her holiday expectations on. It makes a good story to tell around the table, and it also helps her stay on track every time she feels an unreasonable expectation trying to sweet-talk her into inevitable disaster.

CHAPTER 9

A NATION IN MINIATURE

*"Compare the nations of the world to the members of a family.
A family is a nation in miniature. Simply enlarge the circle of the
household, and you have the nation. Enlarge the circle of nations,
and you have all humanity. The conditions surrounding the family
surround the nation. The happenings in the family are
the happenings in the life of the nation."*

—'Abdu'l-Bahá, *The Promulgation of Universal Peace*

My First Teacher Is Still Twenty-One

*Mothers truly are our first teachers, which may explain
why we can feel so inexplicably alone once they're gone.*

My mother didn't have a "real" birthday except during leap years, which means that even when her death certificate recorded her age as eighty, she was still technically only twenty-one.

There were beginning to be discernible signs of age, such as the slight bend in her slender frame, in the months before the sudden heart attack that ended her life. But the challenge her slate-blue eyes tossed back at the world even then always made her seem so much more like a feisty young adult.

Her only grandchildren, our now-adult kids, join us at this time each year for Ayyám-i-Há, a four-day (five in a leap year) holiday we celebrate as a Bahá'í family. These days occur just before a nineteen-day period in which we'll fast during daylight hours and each take a kind of spiritual inventory as we wind down toward a new year that will begin when the spring equinox arrives on March 21st.

It is always especially easy to remember my mother during these happy days, which focus on sharing, hospitality, and reaching out to others. If anyone ever embodied the true spirituality—and joy—of what such acts are really about, my mum sure did.

Mothers truly are our first teachers, which may explain why we can feel so inexplicably alone once they're gone. What they teach will include things we'll eventually come to prize, even if we didn't initially. With each passing year it becomes more obvious how many of the things I value in myself can be traced back to my mother, a military spouse whose life didn't turn out anything like her twenty-one-year-old self imagined it would.

A young British war bride, my mother held down the fort in her family's remote north-England home after the handsome Yank she had married returned to Britain's coast for duty during World War II. During the years my dad was at war, she cared for my older sister, then a newborn, as well as for an elderly relative suffering with cancer, *and* several children who'd been evacuated from London. I recently learned that my newly postpartum, first-time mother also hooked rugs to generate income to compensate for the meager wartime rations on which her crowded household had to subsist.

Having been a young mother myself, I now wonder how she ever found the time to do these things, and I marvel that she took in those young evacuees at all. She knew, however, what kind of life they'd face back home in the city during wartime, because her young face already wore nasty scars from her service as a fire warden during the infamous "Blitzkrieg."

If anyone modeled for me how to welcome change gracefully, it was my mother, who came to a new culture to meet her Boston-Irish in-laws, then proceeded to make a home for her family—over and over—in locations all over the world where her military spouse was stationed. Her deliberate and dedicated "nesting" efforts are some of my oldest memories. They gave every place we lived that consistent feeling of home that I could recognize anywhere, even though we were constantly uprooted and forced to start over in place after place.

Life in a military family meant I had to keep making new friends, and my mother, as with most everything, encouraged me in this endeavor and did her best to turn it into an adventure. She made it easier to nurture friendships by always welcoming playmates at our house and utterly charming them with her warmth. (They usually loved her accent, too.) Friends still talk about how inviting it was at our house, while I grew up believing that's how it was everywhere.

Because she was such a canny yet unobtrusive ally in assisting our friendships, my sister and I now find it easy to make friends wherever we go, to be the one to go talk to someone standing alone at a party, as we often saw her do. With her lively mind, she always had friendly, interesting questions that would gently coax people into the nicest conversations, even if she had to ask them in a language she was struggling to learn.

Long before the days of what the sixties would label women's lib, military spouses like her were already demonstrating women's versatility and capability, strong models for their daughters—and sons. When you're so often the only parent on the scene, there's simply no room for the kind of thinking that's limited by gender bias.

Among other invaluable gifts, she was able to listen in a way that made you feel priceless, like listening to you at that moment was the most important thing in the world. She also taught me how to value and use my own time—not just to be efficient and accomplish things, important as that is, but to also savor and enjoy something worth enjoying.

It makes me more than a little sad that I can so easily recognize these things now that she isn't here to thank in person, but I also know that millions of parents have gone to great lengths for their children and never received the acknowledgment they deserve.

"A father and mother endure the greatest troubles and hardships for their children; and often when the children have reached the age of maturity, the parents pass on to the other world," the Bahá'í writings acknowledge. "Rarely does it happen that a father and mother in this world see the reward of the care and trouble they have undergone for their children. Therefore, children, in return for this care and trouble, must show forth charity and beneficence, and must implore pardon and forgiveness for their parents."[1]

After my mother's death, the one thing I heard most consistently from the many people who loved her was how much kindness and help she had always shown them. It's quite clear, therefore, how I can best honor her memory. Being someone who consistently demonstrated kindness and generosity is likely the most important lesson my first teacher ever gave me.

So, thanks for everything, and happy almost-birthday, Mum. You'll always be twenty-one to me.

A Fortress for Well-Being and Happiness

*In the Bahá'í marriage ceremony, the couple speaks a vow that
makes the marriage a contract of three parties, a contract
that extends well beyond their own life.*

In the last days of my father's life, there was a photo he displayed
prominently in his room at the assisted-living facility. Taken in our
living room a few months before, it showed our daughter radiating a
joy that people continue to remark on. "She looks so *beautiful*," they
often add. Indeed, supreme happiness will do that to a body.

Beside her, gazing back at my photographer husband with a sweet
and soul-baring smile, cheek pressed tenderly against Vanessa's hair,
is Tim, now our son-in-law.

Everyone who entered my father's room was greeted by these two
beaming faces. As visitors and caregivers began visualizing a good
passing for my dad, they probably began holding in their minds an
image of this very happy-looking couple, too. Endings and beginnings
often manifest in just this coinciding way.

My father, as those leaving this world need to do, continued to
withdraw from it in many ways over those last months. But like
a giant sticky note you place somewhere to remember something
important, he kept this photograph where he and everyone could see
it, and he continually called attention to it if you somehow managed
to miss its insistent little ray of light. No matter how absorbed he
may have been in life's final tasks, my dad kept an eye trained on his
granddaughter's future happiness.

I can't remember when our own little household didn't hold an
ever-present consciousness of marriage in a very everyday, benevolent
way. Each of our children, even when very small, would make matter-
of-fact references to their future partners and have continued this
practice as young adults.

Now I know this next assertion will sound especially strange, but
whenever they did this, it seemed as though I could *feel* the presence
of that future family member and that future family. That's the same

way I felt when I first heard my son-in-law's voice on the phone, which happened to occur before our daughter had gotten to know him particularly well. I had that sensation of, "Well, *there* you are. I had a feeling you'd be along soon."

Describing marriage as the foundation of a unified society, Bahá'u'lláh called it "a fortress for well-being and salvation."[2] The Bahá'í writings describe the two parties in a marriage as two wings of a bird that "should be united both physically and spiritually, that they may ever improve the spiritual life of each other, and may enjoy everlasting unity throughout all the worlds of God."[3] So that theirs may be a good flight together, you might say.

Couples are encouraged to strive to become "loving companions and comrades and at one with each other for time and eternity," and, before they enter into marriage, they're advised to "exercise the utmost care to become thoroughly acquainted with the character of the other."[4]

Once they've chosen their partner—a choice that Bahá'í teachings say belongs solely to them—there are three requirements for a Bahá'í marriage. The first is that each party obtains the parents' approval of the marriage. There is no age restriction on this teaching, which means that when my friend Martin wanted to marry again, he still needed the blessing of his nearly ninety-year-old mother. In addition to being a means by which parents might assist and guide the couple, this requirement helps preserve unity within both the marriage and the extended family. It also serves to honor one's parents and the essential spiritual bond between child and parent.

Another requirement for Bahá'í marriage is the presence of two witnesses alongside the couple as they fulfill the third simple requirement, which is to speak the following verse: "We will all, verily, abide by the will of God."[5]

This vow makes the marriage a contract of three parties. And that contract extends beyond the lives of the couple, as my husband and I came to recognize on the day we said our own vows.

"I realized," he told me afterward, "that when I said that, I was referring to the two of us, plus everyone there with us to support our marriage, and our future children."

And indeed, the spiritual resonance of that vow has been with all of us ever since, even in the sound of my son-in-law's voice that first time I heard it.

There are some things we cannot know or understand without the passing of time and the accumulation of experience, as well as reflection on that experience. What I feel more deeply each day is that the commitment of my parents' marriage, the fortress for well-being they sought to forge, and the one my husband and I have endeavored to fashion, resonates in our children's lives now like that vow we spoke twenty-eight years ago.

Along with that photo of Vanessa and Tim, my father also kept a calendar on which he continued to mark a few very significant dates right up until the last three weeks of his life. He didn't have a chance to note our daughter's wedding date, but I have a feeling it was on his "spiritual" calendar. I suspect he may have known it even before she did, since the big proposal originated on Father's Day, shortly after he died.

Each time I'd feel a little nervous about the details of the big day, I'd get an image of him standing beside my mother in something like their own version of that photograph of the new happy couple. And I could hear their reassurance: "Don't worry, Honey. Everything will be just fine. *We will all, verily, abide by the will of God.*"

The Ultimate Fear Factor

Within hours of becoming a mother, I was appalled to discover
my mind envisioning the most dreadful scenes of
potential danger for our new little daughter.

For years I thought my mother had some kind of personality flaw that caused her to imagine every awful thing that could possibly happen to me, as if her mind ran some constant mental version of Lemony Snicket's "A Series of Unfortunate Events." It seemed ridiculous that even after I'd been out in the world on my own, she'd still lie awake worrying about me. All I could think was that she really needed to get a grip.

Then, within hours of becoming a mother myself, I was appalled to discover my mind envisioning the most dreadful scenes of potential danger for our new little daughter. What kind of monster must I be to imagine things like this? Here I simply wanted to cradle this tiny pink bundle in contented bliss, but instead, all these hideous thoughts kept bludgeoning their way in. I figured it must be postpartum exhaustion.

As these scenes continued to hijack my unsuspecting thoughts, I finally confided in a friend about them.

"Oh, THAT," she said with a dismissive wave of her hand obviously meant to reassure me. "You can't help it. Now that you're responsible for someone so helpless, a part of you has shifted into twenty-four-hour vigilance for any possibility of danger."

When I protested that having such things flash through my mind made me feel bad, as though I were somehow responsible for them, she insisted knowingly, "It's normal."

As the years passed and our two children grew increasingly mobile, my mind's little screen of horrors began a pattern of looping in on itself to replay scenes of things that had *almost* happened. There were numerous such rewinds of our four-year-old son's shout of, "Hey, Mom! Look!" when he dangled by one hand at the top of a slide at least twelve feet tall. In another frequent rerun, I'm struggling to cut open a box when our daughter, then six, suddenly appears beside me at the foot of our basement stairs brandishing the largest carving knife we own and chirruping, "Will this help?" Beyond making it down those stairs safely with this terrifying object, she'd also had to climb up (and subsequently down) a counter to retrieve it from a rack mounted on the side of a kitchen cabinet—all in well under a minute. The dreadful potential ramifications of that scene still play in my head—and she's now twenty-six.

Stage by developmental stage I watched our kids move off into their own lives. With the advent of their driver's licenses, I simply couldn't fathom how I'd ever been so callous and exasperated about my own mother's requests (made even after I had children of my own) that I call her after I'd arrived home safely. What arrogance of mine had scoffed at her lying awake until she'd heard my car in the driveway or heard my bedroom door close? How hadn't it all made complete sense to me all along?

My empathy deepened, of course, as our nest began to empty. In the case of our oldest child, it was as though a hurricane upended it overnight. Twelve hours after her high-school graduation, her father and I stood in the driveway in our pajamas waving her off as she struck out in her fully packed, aging Volvo for an internship on a North Carolina farm. When she was finally able to find a phone in that rural setting, nearly three days had passed and somehow I had actually managed to live through them. So when, short of becoming part of the space program, she next went as far away from home as she possibly could to live and work in China, I was pretty well conditioned for letting go.

I know today that if it hadn't been for a couple of very important discoveries, I'd have disintegrated under the weight of the world's hardest role, whose job description seems to demand holding your children as closely as you can while simultaneously letting them go.

Early on, one of many wise friends who had survived this dilemma reminded me that, whatever my own personal faith happened to be or not be, greater forces besides my own were at work in our children's lives. A kind companion during some rocky hours, she managed to impress on me the fact that life would feel a whole lot better each time I stopped and remembered this. And it does.

Another undeniably helpful strategy—one that's useful anyway if you're trying to practice parental vigilance—is to learn how to be more present in the moments you're already in. How I wish I'd learned this sooner. It's one of the very best parenting gifts to offer our kids. It automatically increases our ability to draw on the resources within ourselves, beyond ourselves, and also the ones that are treasured within our children.

One of my most instructive moments came when my son, who had the opportunity to do some physical labor that could also be dangerous, met my eyes earnestly as he acknowledged my concern for him and urged, "I can *do* this, Mom." The unspoken remainder of that plea was "Please believe in me."

Bahá'u'lláh writes, "In the treasuries of the knowledge of God there lieth concealed a knowledge which, when applied, will largely, though not wholly, eliminate fear."[6] This knowledge, He adds, should be taught from childhood, as it will greatly aid in the elimination of fear. "Whatever decreaseth fear increaseth courage,"[7] He reminds.

One of the big gifts our children offered me as a mother was that invitation to let go of fear, to surrender worry in order to be as fully present as possible in both their lives and my own.

Even though some of those Lemony Snicket scenes still creep into my head every once in a while (I'll always be a mom, after all), I can also see how they began to diminish the more I tried to express my personal faith by believing in our kids and in life itself.

The Big Picture Always Holds the Most Possibilities

As parents, we want to remember that we're teaching children,
not just teaching lessons.

I've recently had a few chances to witness what I call "Circumstantial Parental Myopia," a tendency to miss the big picture when it comes to our children. If I can recognize it, it's only because, regrettably, I've had so many chances to experience it myself.

A ten-year-old friend of our family named Stacey was really excited about baking a cake to surprise her parents. In fact, she was so intent on getting it made while they were out that she created quite a mess in the kitchen. When her parents arrived home, she could barely contain herself. Her big, loud "Surprise!" probably made their hearts jump.

Her mother, nursing a headache, was relieved to have the visit she and Stacey's father had just made to an ailing relative behind her. When Stacey gestured happily to the table where a slightly lumpy, somewhat distorted layer cake sat, all her mother saw was the array of used cups, bowls, and utensils strewn across the kitchen.

"What have you DONE?" she cried. "How could you make such a mess?"

Stacey tried to explain, but there wasn't room for her words in her mother's angry reaction. "I should make you clean it up this instant, but I'm too tired to stay up and make sure you do it right. You get to bed, and take care of this first thing in the morning," she snapped and stalked off to bed herself.

In the moments that followed, Stacey and her father looked silently at each other in her mother's wake. Stacey was probably going to shed lots of tears that night. Her father told her, "I'm sorry, Sweetheart. She never even saw your wonderful cake," as he put his arm around her.

We can all empathize with what Stacey felt. Most parents can also relate to what it's like when in-our-face problems blind us from seeing the things that will have far more significance in the long run. Messes can definitely be an unwelcome intrusion. But messes can be cleaned up, while it's very difficult to retrieve a child's sense of dignity after it's been transgressed.

Children certainly need to learn responsibility and accept the consequences of their choices and actions. But as parents, we want to remember that we're teaching children, not just teaching lessons. Keeping the big picture in view involves many things, including understanding where our children's intentions and motivations may lie and being considerate of their feelings. It means being able to spot and leverage an opportunity for their development when it arises, rather than stepping in its way.

Had Stacey's mother been able to see beyond her own situation and catch the spirit of her daughter's love-filled gift, she might have been able to tell her nearly the same thing in a different way: "Thank you for the cake. I think we're both too tired to clean up tonight. But first thing tomorrow, that's what you'll need to do, OK?"

A friend told me about another cake and another case of "Circumstantial Parental Myopia." In this case, the parent's opportunity to let her child learn something was foiled by her desire to rush in and save him.

My friend was cutting her son's cake at his birthday party when a child bolted in front of the others to be served first. As intervention, the birthday boy's mother said, "Why yes, I'd LOVE for you to help," and enlisted his help with serving cake to the other guests. He was doing this willingly when his mother, thinking he might be disappointed, stepped in and took his place. In her well-meaning effort to spare him frustration, she short-circuited his chance to learn more about the pleasure of serving others.

No one gets through a parenting lifetime without bouts of "Circumstantial Parental Myopia." Most occur when our vision is obstructed by how things affect us personally, or may affect what others think of us.

As parents, we'll always encounter messes to clean up, or moments when our children's behavior can be potentially distressing or embarrassing. But if our child, the person, is what we see first, we'll also see the circumstances around us more clearly and take the time to discover what the very best response may be.

CHAPTER 10

AN INFUSION OF MIGHTY GRACE

"This is the Day in which God's most excellent favors have been poured out upon men, the Day in which His most mighty grace hath been infused into all created things. It is incumbent upon all the peoples of the world to reconcile their differences, and, with perfect unity and peace, abide beneath the shadow of the Tree of His care and loving-kindness."

—Bahá'u'lláh, *Gleanings from the Writings of Bahá'u'lláh*

Fastening My Eyes on Glimpses of Heaven

*A day can become something quite remarkable when fasting frees us
from the usual daily rhythm that food so often imposes upon it.*

I keep catching myself lately as I start to make a lunch or coffee date,
my favorite way to visit and catch up with friends.

"Oh, yeah," I usually remember aloud. "I don't eat during most
of March."

"You don't *eat?*" My listener's tone is invariably shocked.

"Oh, well, yes, I do. Just not during daylight hours."

For the nineteen days that fall between March 2nd and 20th, I'm one
of a few million members of the Bahá'í Faith around the world who
wake up early to have our breakfast before sunrise and then abstain
from food and drink until sunset. Knowing how especially fond I am
of eating, friends often express real sympathy when I get to this part
of the explanation.

I don't know how to tell them that I sometimes find myself wishing
that this annual fast lasted even longer than it does. Sure, it can be
an inconvenience in day-to-day terms, and it can tax me physically
and make some social situations a bit awkward; but a day can become
something quite remarkable when its usual daily rhythm is freed from
the demands that food so often imposes upon it. And the slowing of
my own pace that the fast necessitates, together with the prayer and
reflection it inspires, opens doors to many sweet surprises that make
my soul feel very well fed indeed.

People of most faiths fast—some for a day at a time; some for a
full lunar month, as faithful Muslims do. Like many religions, the
Bahá'í Faith sees great value in the practice of fasting as a discipline
for both body and soul.

But it's the soul part that is so inviting for me each year, even
when my body protests a bit at what is roughly a twelve-hour wait
between meals. This fast occurs in the weeks that precede the spring
equinox, which Bahá'ís celebrate as the beginning of a new year.
The fast itself is viewed as a time for taking a spiritual inventory
as we prepare to embark on a new year. Its significance is therefore

essentially spiritual in character, with abstinence from food and drink acting as a symbolic reminder of the importance of abstaining from preoccupation with one's self and the world. It's a reminder that we are, first and foremost, spiritual beings.

Because the primary aim of the fast is spiritual reflection and regeneration, everyone can participate, whether they're able to abstain from food or not. Those excused from fasting include women who are pregnant, menstruating, or nursing a child; those who are ill, engaged in heavy labor, in the midst of a journey; and those under the age of fifteen or over the age of seventy. (However, one eighty-four-year-old friend looks forward to the fast each year just as much as I do.)

One of the things I love about this period is that it enhances a sense of conscious awareness for me, and that always leads to unexpected glimpses of heaven right here on earth.

"Fasting is the cause of awakening man," the Bahá'í writings say. "The heart becomes tender and the spirituality of man increases. This is produced by the fact that man's thoughts will be confined to the commemoration of God, and through this awakening and stimulation surely ideal advancements follow."[1]

One friend who's also fasting is Ronnie, whose work involves accompanying brain-injured clients to a local day program. Their activities are held in a large community building shared by several service organizations.

One day recently, a client who had been hit by a car as a child was being fed his lunch by his caregiver in the building's cafeteria. Food was dripping down his chin onto his bib, and he was in no position to clean his own face or even ask for it to be cleaned, as he has little control over any of the movements of his body.

But he has total control over his heart, Ronnie says.

He has become the friend of a group of preschoolers who attend a school in the same building. Each day, after the children finish their lunch, they crowd around their friend's wheelchair and tell him all about their day. They aren't the least bit bothered by the fact that he is unable to answer them or that bits of food fall off his bib onto the floor. After all, they often have the same problem.

One day recently, as Ronnie watched this little group interact, he felt like he had suddenly spotted one of those glimpses of heaven. The small, enthusiastic voices were regaling the young man in the wheelchair, and he was sitting quietly, as he has no choice but to do.

And then, in the next unexpected moment, he raised one of his sometimes erratically moving arms and settled it softly on a little girl's shoulder, like a broken-winged bird. Then she smiled up at him and he smiled down at her.

Life is made up of moments, and some of those moments are pure heaven, Ronnie says. But you need to look carefully for them because sometimes they happen in a crowded lunchroom and if you are always looking up, or down, or somewhere else distractedly, you just might miss them.

Fortunately, he adds, life is very generous with the portions of these that it dishes out—a veritable feast, whether you happen to be fasting or not.

A Season for Happiness

*"Spring flowers remind us to be happy. It's as though God treasured
this invitation in each one and then spread them abundantly
about the landscape to ensure we wouldn't miss it."*

One year I celebrated three New Year's Days in as many months.
While living in Shanghai, China, I was surprised to learn that the
traditional New Year's Day celebrated in the Western world would
also be a day off for me in my new home. (This after I had seen the
city decked out for Christmas in a manner worthy of a Dickens story,
yet the day itself had been business-as-usual.)

Then, about six weeks later in February, I got to experience the
unforgettable weeklong party that is Chinese New Year in China. If
I ever have another chance, I'll definitely invest in a set of earplugs,
though. Even the more meager firecrackers that many of our
neighbors set off to drive away gloomy or bad spirits and welcome in
a prosperous year were fairly deafening.

Upon my arrival back in the States, I transitioned into my American
life with one of the highlights of my year—the annual fast that millions
of Bahá'ís follow for nineteen days during daylight hours each March.
It's a kind of spiritual preparation, reflection, and stock-taking time
that precedes Naw-Rúz (meaning "New Day"), which marks the new
year on the Bahá'í calendar. The Bahá'í New Year begins with the
vernal equinox on March 21st, the first day of spring.

'Abdu'l-Bahá has provided one of my favorite descriptions of the
spiritual significance of Naw-Rúz. He says,

> At the time of the vernal equinox in the material world a wonderful
> vibrant energy and new life-quickening is observed everywhere
> in the vegetable kingdom; the animal and human kingdoms are
> resuscitated and move forward with a new impulse. The whole
> world is born anew, resurrected. Gentle zephyrs are set in motion,
> wafting and fragrant; flowers bloom; the trees are in blossom, the
> air temperate and delightful; how pleasant and beautiful become
> the mountains, fields and meadows. Likewise, the spiritual bounty

and springtime of God quicken the world of humanity with a new animus and vivification. All the virtues which have been deposited and potential in human hearts are being revealed from that Reality as flowers and blossoms from divine gardens. It is a day of joy, a time of happiness, a period of spiritual growth. I beg of God that this divine spiritual civilization may have the fullest impression and effect upon you. May you become as growing plants. May the trees of your hearts bring forth new leaves and variegated blossoms. May ideal fruits appear from them in order that the world of humanity, which has grown and developed in material civilization, may be quickened in the bringing forth of spiritual ideals. Just as human intellects have revealed the secrets of matter and have brought forth from the realm of the invisible the mysteries of nature, may minds and spirits, likewise, come into the knowledge of the verities of God, and the realities of the Kingdom be made manifest in human hearts.[2]

Each time I read that passage, I envision a brilliant, variegated hillside bursting into bloom all of a sudden, just as so many settings will when spring arrives, despite the unpredictability of the meteorological scene these days.

I'm also reminded of one of the earliest Naw-Rúz celebrations that our family shared together. The happiness of that day, and the spiritual promise that Naw-Rúz unfailingly holds each year, were captured for me in a photograph I snapped of our then kindergarten-age son. At the time, we were packing up our small Toyota to head for the Naw-Rúz party that night. I opened a car door to find him sitting in the backseat so surrounded by a massive bouquet of daffodils in full bloom that I could barely see him.

We were bringing these flowers to decorate the rented hall where about fifty of us would celebrate that night, and my husband, in order to ensure that the flowers would arrive safely, had given our small son the very important task of holding them as we rode. He had never seen these harbingers of spring before and was obviously delighted with them and with this special assignment. It's hard to remember which made the bigger impact, that explosion of yellow blooms or the hugeness of his delighted smile as he grinned back at me, clutching his precious cargo.

In their very essence, daffodils, like so many spring flowers, remind us to be happy. It's as though God treasured this special invitation in each one and then spread them abundantly about the landscape to make sure we wouldn't miss it.

Through the years, whenever I look at this sweet image of our son in his early Naw-Rúz delight, I recall that wish of 'Abdu'l-Bahá's: "May you become as growing plants. May the trees of your hearts bring forth new leaves and variegated blossoms."

Indeed, may each new springtime remind us that we are spiritual beings, however earthly our journey often seems.

Wisdom That Arrives on Wings and Paws

The sun was barely up, and the animal kingdom already had me humbled and thankful—two things that are usually very good for me.

They've done it again, those animals, gone and left their tracks all over my heart. I must have broadcast the message that my heart was in need of a bit of softening, even humility, and in rushed a flock of wings and flurry of hooves in response.

It all started when I spent a few days at my friend Anna's farm, hoping to advance a writing project with a deadline looming closer day by day. While humans and civilization were scarce, animal life, and its gifts and lessons, seemed to be everywhere.

Two doe-eyed cows supplied the cream for my coffee while a pair of errant, curious chickens obligingly left my morning's eggs in some nearby hay. On my way back from the barn, I noticed that the turkeys had cleverly availed themselves of the convenient perch afforded by my nearby car while the guinea fowl scampered around it in small, noisy crowds. My friend tells me that these birds are so sociable that when one of them is broody or ailing, the entire group pays her visits.

In a nearby pen, a mother goat angled her body against the rear of a low shed in order to scratch her back, and the two tiny kids trailing behind her did exactly the same. Imitation still seems to be the predominant way many of us learn, particularly the smaller ones.

As I was savoring my homegrown omelet, the farmhouse door appeared to swing open on its own and in strode Lane, one of the trio of dogs that comprise the farm's twenty-four-hour welcoming committee. "That's a tough one to open," his owner observed about the latch-handled door. And if Lane's executing this feat with his front paw seems a wonder, the fact that he has only three legs is a sobering reminder should I feel tempted to dwell on any limitations of my own.

Yes, the sun was barely up, and the animal kingdom already had me humbled and thankful—two things that are usually very good for me. But the jackpot was still to come, lurking in a documentary I'd later watch about a former circus elephant named Shirley. After a long day at the keyboard, I decided that would be my downtime and reward.

Forty minutes after the film ended I was still racked by sobs. Shirley's is a long story. And I'm a sucker for triumph-in-adversity tales, especially when the adversity part goes into hard, grueling overtime. But I had no idea that I even still knew how to cry in that gulping, nonstop way that my two-year-old friends do.

Shirley had toughed it out for a long time, enduring for decades a life that delivered the precise opposite of everything an elephant is designed to experience and receive in life. The mere body language of captives like Shirley usually makes plain just how dispiriting they find their circumstances.

Early in life, she'd been savaged by another elephant and left permanently damaged and scarred in a way that made you wince to look at her. The incident was the result of human error, but Shirley's punishment was that she'd never had contact with another member of her species since. And what have zoologists finally discovered in recent years that elephants yearn for most? Why, exactly that kind of company, of course. It isn't as though they've been keeping it a secret.

Shirley's story would have seemed unforgivably harsh had it not been for the kind caretaker, now fairly elderly himself, who'd remained her friend long after he'd retired from the job that brought them together. At the time the documentary was made, the heightened conflict in the story was that Shirley was about to lose this one last friend as she was shipped off to some sort of retirement home for circus elephants. The caretaker wasn't even sure how he was going to survive it himself, and he felt darn sure that Shirley wouldn't.

I was crying quite freely and fiercely at this point in the documentary, no doubt moved by a seemingly unceasing chain of events that had conspired in Shirley's life to keep her lonely. I was outraged and saddened at how human ignorance had resulted in repeated suffering and sacrifice for her. The fact that she had been marooned without the very thing that might have made it all bearable—companionship— seemed the most wrenching of all.

But mercifully, there was some unexpected reprieve and redemption in this story. The day that Shirley was transferred to her new home, another younger elephant arrived the same day. It turns out that this was an orphan that Shirley had nurtured way back in her circus days, someone she'd taken under her trunk, so to speak.

Folks had brought the two elephants together with hopes of reuniting them, yet also had trepidation about whether they'd get along, so the two were placed in separate adjacent stalls on the first night before they'd potentially be released into a big pasture together the next day.

Thankfully, the scene that showed their first encounter that night had little narration. Any human input at that point would have felt like taking a flash photo in a very sacred place. The movements of the animals themselves were language enough.

Despite the bars that separated them, the two tenderly embraced each other with their trunks for long hours into the night, each making soft, soothing sounds. I don't know what Shirley was or wasn't feeling after those dozens of lonely years, but I know that this certainly opened up a gusher in my heart.

"Upon the inmost reality of each and every created thing He hath shed the light of one of His names, and made it a recipient of the glory of one of His attributes,"[3] Bahá'u'lláh says in describing how the Creator fashioned all creation. At a time when we see relationships of all kinds breaking down around us, all of God's creation, especially the animals, can provide lessons for our benefit every day, if we remember to pay attention.

Try to Leave the Light On

Every once in a while, a piece of truth that's been
looking me in the face for years, making no attempt
to hide itself, literally stops me in my tracks.

From the time of my earliest memories, I've been attracted to the concept that one universal light of truth is found in all of the world's religions. It's still baffling to me how religious intolerance could grow so powerful and destructive when the illumination from that light is so unfailingly consistent and bright. As one friend pointed out recently: "What's so hard to understand about the oneness of truth? The light from the lamp I turn on back home is the same as the one here on your table. If it's that basic a truth materially speaking, why would it be any different spiritually?"

Bahá'u'lláh addresses the nature and power of this light not only within religious revelation, but also within each soul. In a collection of His writings called the Hidden Words He says,

O Son of Being! With the hands of power I made thee and with the fingers of strength I created thee; and within thee have I placed the essence of My light.[4]

O Son of Being! Thou art My lamp and My light is in thee. Get thou from it thy radiance and seek none other than Me. For I have created thee rich and have bountifully shed my favor upon thee.[5]

Every once in a while, a piece of truth that's been looking me in the face for years, certainly making no attempt to hide itself, stops me in my tracks. Usually it's some kind of coincidence or recent life experience that sounds an inner chord and makes words that I think I've heard and known for a long time suddenly come through with new implications as loud as a siren.

An experience I had in the dark a few weeks ago gave me a whole new appreciation for light and lamps—any purveyor of light in general.

My husband and I had rented a small and delightful "Ferien-wohnung" or vacation apartment in Germany, close to where friends of ours live. The kind landlord had shown us around the place briefly before he headed away on business. His English was limited, as was our German. What I later realized he had cautioned us about as he gave us the key to the front door was, roughly translated, "Remember the light."

When we returned home later that night, it quickly became obvious why he'd said this. We had neglected to put on the exterior light. And on this overcast night, the narrow old-town streets, most of which are also hills, were incredibly dark. The uneven, irregularly spaced steps down into the tiny alley on which our quarters' front door was situated were treacherous. We groped our way down very slowly and carefully in the thick blackness, as the cobbles were also quite slippery underfoot from the cold rain. We were relieved to finally step inside without any sprains or falls.

The very next morning, I read those two Hidden Words. The angels definitely have their fun with me that way sometimes.

And to launch my reflection further, there was a third piece of guidance to go with them: *"The good pleasure of God is love for His creatures. The will and plan of God is that each individual member of humankind shall become illumined like unto a lamp, radiant with all the destined virtues of humanity, leading his fellow creatures out of natural darkness into the heavenly light. Therein rests the virtue and glory of the world of humanity."* [6]

One light, and so very many lamps—each and every member of humankind. That's quite a supply. How might we feed our own lamp to special brightness? Just what kind of brilliant light might all of those "destined virtues of humanity" provide that makes it bright enough to lead us from the "natural darkness" of a sore-tried world into the safe, joyful freedom of "heavenly light"?

CHAPTER 11

TENDER PLANTS

"I am a tender plant; cause me to be nurtured through the outpourings of the clouds of Thy bounty."

—'Abdu'l-Bahá, *Bahá'í Prayers*

Animals Help Us Know Our Humanity

*Children's hearts are especially tender when young, and animals
seem tailor-made to nurture caring qualities within them.*

When asked about his children's experience during the year his family
spent touring the world, David Elliot Cohen, author of *One Year Off,*
said that what most helped his children relate to the many cultures they
saw were the animals. While foreign settings sometimes overwhelmed
their young sensibilities, any animal, wild or domesticated, would
immediately capture their attention and ground them in a sense of
connection with their surroundings.

Children and animals seem to be one of life's most inevitable combina-
tions. Animals populate the vast majority of kids' books and other
media and are the most common decorative designs on children's
clothing, furniture, and toys. People often compliment a pet's nature
by noting how gentle it is even around rambunctious children.

Experts agree that interaction with animals gives children the chance
to acquire many different kinds of knowledge and develop two especially
important qualities—responsibility and kindness. Studies have also
demonstrated how humane education that teaches kindness to animals
can affect the way that children learn to relate to people. Most violent
criminals have a history of childhood cruelty to animals.

When parents help children learn to care for animals responsibly,
those children often grow up to be good coworkers, spouses, and
parents. When parents don't make this effort, lots of animals wind
up in shelters and another generation misses the chance to acquire
some essential life skills.

Within the teachings of the Bahá'í Faith, treating animals with
kindness is a matter of great importance and an easy one to introduce
into children's spiritual education. Humane education about animals
helps children develop an appreciation and concern for all of life
as they practice and develop the qualities of empathy, awareness,
compassion, and care—qualities without which most human
relationships wither. Children's hearts are especially tender when
young, and animals seem tailor-made to foster caring and loving
qualities within them.

The act of caring for animals also enhances children's environmental education by helping them understand the web of life in which every living thing is connected to every other living thing on the planet. As children learn to make decisions, the development of compassion for those in need can lead them to ethical decisions that take into account other people, animals, and the environment.

One ten-year-old friend of mine demonstrated an interesting understanding of this interrelationship. He longed to have a dog, but his older brother's severe allergies prevented that possibility. His parents encouraged him to save for a bike he'd been admiring instead and gave him some money to help him start saving for it. For several months he did odd jobs to keep that savings fund growing.

One day, he went with friends to a local humane society where he saw many animals in need of homes. When his friends' family brought home two cats, he felt sad that he couldn't help by bringing an animal home, too.

The next day, he asked his mother whether they could drive over to the shelter after school. When she reminded him that they couldn't have a dog or cat and tried to discourage the trip, he told her there was something important he needed to do there.

After school the next day, he raced to his room and brought out the jar with his savings. His mother told me she had tears in her eyes as they took that ride to the shelter to deliver his gift.

A few days later, the boy got a call from a young couple in his neighborhood who had been very moved when a shelter staff member had shared with them the story of this boy's spontaneous generosity. The couple had also been very concerned about leaving their dog alone all day while both of them worked and wondered whether my young friend would like to earn money by spending time with their pet.

He'd have gladly done this gratis, of course, but as he played with his furry new friend after school each day, his savings jar gradually filled up again. In his love for animals, he found a step he could take, and it led to one of the most rewarding discoveries that interaction with animals can teach—that the reciprocal cycle of life is truly designed to meet everyone's needs.

Confidants Build Confidence

Young people navigating the stormy waters toward maturity need trusted advisors with more life experience than their peers. And they don't always want them to be their parents.

When our daughter was fourteen, I saw her sitting on a park bench across from our house talking to a family friend.

She'd asked this retired school principal for his listening ear because something was troubling her that she preferred not to talk about with us. And she knew she needed to talk to someone.

To our inevitable "Why not us?" she responded, after an evident struggle to summon patience, "Because you've told me it's important not to talk about other people's business."

We learned that the concern she'd shared involved a friend who was making choices that made our daughter uncomfortable and confused about how to respond.

When I told her, "You could have talked with us about it without saying who it was," she, with one of those eye-rolling expressions parents elicit so easily in fourteen-year-olds, said, "But you'd have known. You just would."

My parental pleas about safety and "What if something terrible had happened?" must have really taxed her patience as she assured, "Mom! I'd have talked to you if it was that bad."

And I knew it was true. That she'd acquired such regard for confidentiality by this age, and was even willing to give us a little credit for it astonished me. But what the incident drove home most was how much young people navigating the stormy waters of their teenage years need trusted confidants who have more life experience than their peers. And they don't always want them to be their parents.

All of us, whatever our age, benefit from the kind of listening that helps us think out loud. Sometimes we invite feedback and gain insights, but the mere act of sharing a concern helps us remember we have the ability to find the answer, either within or outside of ourselves.

Linda Kavelin Popov, coauthor of *The Family Virtues Guide*, defines confidence as "having faith in something or someone. It is a kind of trust. When you have self-confidence, you trust that you have what it takes to handle whatever happens. When you are confident in others, you count on them. Confidence brings the strength to try new things."

Naturally, we want our children to gain this valuable asset. But why limit their resources to just us? Adolescents already have so much going on that's confusing. Part of that pulling (even pushing) away they do with parents is surely some developmental recognition that a.) It's a big world and I need to be part of it; and b.) The more I do, the more resources I'll find to grow. Of course, teenagers may not actually voice this belief, but it's in there somewhere.

In former times an extended community of family and others gave young people more places to turn to as they matured, more potential confidants with some life experience to serve as resources for things they didn't necessarily want to broach with their parents—at least not the first time around. Everyone needs these in order to develop autonomy and still feel there are those who will care—and take them seriously. So much of the destructive behavior that entraps youth is attributable to the sense of isolation, even alienation, they feel when they don't have these things.

How can we ensure this kind of network exists for our own children and others? Kavelin Popov suggests we find ways to "cultivate a village mind" to help round up resources for kids. A village offers four gifts: kinship, friendship, mentorship, and worship. In the third, the wisdom and compassion of elders mentors young people into maturity, hears their young dreams, gives them faith in more than themselves, and teaches them the meaning of life. "The future belongs to those who give the next generation reason for hope,"[1] Pierre Teilhard de Chardin once observed.

Most parents are already pretty overwhelmed by what they have to handle and can benefit from some added support from others in the pursuit of their children's education, particularly their spiritual education. Both kinship and worship communities are often a resource for children's education.

Families can also combine resources and efforts to offer this kind of "village community" of support. Recognizing this, some families even plan inexpensive camping vacations together to extend the family circle, experience jointly the inspiration often reflected in the natural world, and develop a wider network of adult mentors for their kids.

Schools can be another source of such mentors, not necessarily through often-overworked teachers, but through the various types of volunteers, coaches, and advisors youth encounter in a variety of activities. I'll forever be grateful to two insightful coaches for the inner and outer guidance they offered each of our children to help them find their way into a deeper awareness of who they really are, well beyond what they were also able to achieve athletically. Might this not also be a fine reason to bring more senior volunteers into our schools?

As parents strive to help develop such resources in their families' and children's lives, they'll find that what goes around also comes around. For years I heard dedicated parents sing the praises of making their home a welcome gathering place for their kids' friends. By default this often results in opportunities for the hosting parents to become recipients of the confidences of those young souls who feel welcomed there.

Our daughter once told a troubled friend, "Oh, go talk to my mother about it. She loves to try to figure that stuff out." That friend, now a delightful young woman, probably taught me more than she gained from our chats, and I still love to hear every new triumph in her life.

None of us really accomplishes anything alone. The sooner we help our children understand this and how to find those places where help and spiritual companionship reside, the faster we get to watch their confidence grow.

Foster the Very Best They Can Be

*Some of the best authorities on what promotes children's
spiritual development are those who give their time
to helping other people's children.*

My days on the perpetual learning curve of parenthood leave me
convinced that the most important gifts parents provide for kids can't
be gift-wrapped, but they're often overshadowed by all the things
that can be.

In fact, some of the best guidance I've heard about the most valuable
gifts for kids comes from those who give their time to helping other
people's children. For example, one parole officer I know strongly
recommends developing a lifestyle that commits to being present
each day in children's lives and to knowing your children like they're
your favorite subject in life. Many parents give their kids less genuine
time than they do a thirty-minute news program. Know everything
you can about your kids, he urges, from what they like and dislike to
how they express feelings.

And, he encourages, make a habit of looking into their eyes—
daily. In his line of work, this is obviously one way to detect drug
use and other activities, but it's also an important means of making
real emotional contact as well as watching for changes and being
equipped to respond.

Along the way, he says, you want kids to learn how to surround
themselves with the kind of people that they want to be like and would
benefit from being like. This requires some thoughtful discussion at
home about things such as qualities of character and behavior, he
says, rather than focusing on the material possessions and social or
celebrity status that seem to get so much air time in everyone's lives
these days.

Don't rescue your child from the natural consequences of poor
choices, he warns. If you only follow one piece of his advice, he
says, make it this: If kids break rules and laws or make other bad
choices, suffering follows. "Nice" parents protect children from many
of life's difficulties and thus rob them of opportunities to develop

independence and responsibility. They take forgotten lunches to school, pay fines for overdue library books, and give up too easily when kids don't follow through on chores or instructions.

Also knowledgeable about bringing out the best in children are many of those folks who care enough to parent children other than their own. Wise, experienced foster parents consistently point out that the path to success in every type of parenting is to observe and gain an understanding of a child's basic nature, his or her style in approaching life and responding to the world. This is such an essential starting place that trying to do anything in our children's lives, or our own, without it may be a big part of why so many of our good intentions fail. Once we gain an understanding of this, we can adjust our interactions—and expectations—and encourage children to leverage their strengths and altruistic qualities to offset the areas in their lives that still need work.

We can enhance our awareness of our children through another indispensable part of the parenting life—spending individual time with a child daily as well as emphasizing sincerely how much we look forward to it. This is a vital way not only to actualize the previous suggestion, but also to build trust and the kind of rapport we'll come to rely on during the tougher times. One foster mom's advice: Try to make it an activity that costs little or nothing, gets you outside, if possible, and includes the opportunity to laugh together.

Successful foster parents also learn early the value of providing children with lots of opportunities to help and to serve, a prime way to "build good spiritual capital," according to one parent. Children want to do this innately when they're small, but many parents miss this prime opportunity to nurture them into responsible, caring, and effective people. They often overlook this precious impulse in children, then try to drag it out of them after it's been discouraged, ignored, or thwarted for years.

Another approach that helps build such spiritual capital is to develop the habit of catching kids in the act of behaving favorably, kind of like a treasure hunt, advises a mother of three who has also parented four foster children. Act as if you expect the best in them and are actually looking to find that treasure. If they make poor choices, let your own sincere (yet non-chastising) disappointment be their greatest deterrent to doing that again, she says.

A major tool of effective parenting that many foster parents identify is that of persistent encouragement. Like adults, children respond to favorable comments and are likely to adopt behaviors that gain them positive attention. It's estimated that kids hear seventeen negative comments at home for every piece of praise or encouragement they receive and, ironically, the brain can't follow or act on negative information. Imagine following directions that tell you: "Don't turn left. Don't take the second road." We'd be lost before we begin, just as many children are. A great place to insert encouragement is when we interact with children first thing in the morning and at the end of each day. Research shows that this also reinforces a child's capacity to absorb the message's positive effects.

Other ways to wield the power of speech wisely are to offer reminders no more than once and then reinforce consequences if children do not cooperate. This, together with actually lowering and calming your voice when you want others to pay attention, proves effective where nagging and yelling never do. One veteran foster parent notes, "Nagging's a huge waste of time and energy and is really just an 'adult' form of whining."

Speaking positively of others, whether family members or those outside the home, or not speaking of others at all is the safest course. One foster parent describes how any kind of negative focus on others usually becomes a source of greater negativity in her household and her life. Like attracts like. But her kids' behavior improved measurably once their parents made the commitment to eliminate negative talk from their family's life.

Finally, one of the most valuable things parents can give their children is consistency, both in routine and with discipline. This is probably the toughest aspect of parenting yet the one that yields the biggest and often the fastest results. The more developed a family's structure and boundaries are, and the more parents uphold these together, the easier it is, says one foster father.

"Scientists make discoveries by knowing what limits have been established and then testing them to see which hold and which can be expanded," he says. "Human beings, especially young ones, do pretty much the same. As so many episodes of 'Supernanny' seem to point out, routine, expectations, and consistency are usually the missing pieces in many struggling families."

Some of the best gifts we have to share with each other are to acknowledge and encourage the best in each other. And whether or not we have the things we thought we would, we always have the moment right in front of us, and what we can offer to each other within it. As the popular saying reminds: "Yesterday's history, tomorrow's a mystery, today is a gift. That's why it's called the present."

CHAPTER 12

THE COUNTENANCE OF BEAUTY

"Say: This is the Paradise on whose foliage the wine of utterance hath imprinted the testimony: 'He that was hidden from the eyes of men is revealed, girded with sovereignty and power!' This is the Paradise, the rustling of whose leaves proclaims: 'O ye that inhabit the heavens and the earth! There hath appeared what hath never previously appeared. He Who, from everlasting, had concealed His Face from the sight of creation is now come.' From the whispering breeze that wafteth amidst its branches there cometh the cry: 'He Who is the sovereign Lord of all is made manifest. The Kingdom is God's,' while from its streaming waters can be heard the murmur: 'All eyes are gladdened, for He Whom none hath beheld, Whose secret no one hath discovered, hath lifted the veil of glory, and uncovered the countenance of Beauty.'"

—Bahá'u'lláh, *Gleanings from the Writings of Bahá'u'lláh*

Gate to the Glory of God

*The Báb began the spiritual revolution
the whole world was waiting for.*

"His life is one of the most magnificent examples of courage which it has been the privilege of mankind to behold," said nineteenth-century writer A. L. M. Nicolas of the Báb.

Each year, on October 20th, Bahá'ís worldwide suspend work and school in memory of someone once described as "matchless in His meekness" and "imperturbable in His serenity."[1] These words describe the Báb, Who started a spiritual revolution in the mid-1800s that resulted in the creation of the Bahá'í Faith.

It's fairly easy to summarize the essence of the Bahá'í Faith, whose central themes are the oneness of God, of religion, and of humanity. But it's harder to explain why the Bahá'í Faith, the youngest of the world's independent monotheistic religions, accepts not one but two new Prophets as representatives of God's voice in our time.

Raised with a deep love for Christ that I hold to this day, I, like other Bahá'ís, see a parallel between the Báb and John the Baptist, who heralded Christ's advent.

Many of us became Bahá'ís because we felt a love for God and religion, and because we felt in our hearts there was "something more." We didn't want to abandon any faith we already had; yet we couldn't help but feel that God's Messengers, including Jesus, Muḥammad, and Buddha, weren't intended to be competing factions. Instead, They can be seen as part of a single, progressive process through which God guides humanity forward. The teachings of the Bahá'í Faith show how the world's major religions are united. And it all began with the Báb.

His story is like a brief, intense storm that reshapes a landscape overnight, or what some have likened to the coming of a "thief in the night." Born Siyyid 'Alí-Muḥammad in 1819 in what was then called Persia, the Báb lived in a time of millennial zeal in which many Christians and Muslims held an expectation that scriptural prophecies were about to be fulfilled.

The Báb was orphaned early in life and was raised by his maternal uncle, who one day was told by his nephew's teacher, an esteemed cleric, that there was nothing more he could teach his prodigious and unfailingly courteous pupil.

"I commit him to your vigilant protection," the teacher told the uncle. "He is not to be treated as a mere child, for in Him I can already discern evidences of that mysterious power which the Revelation of the Ṣáḥibu'z-Zamán* alone can reveal."[2]

In May of 1844 Siyyid 'Alí-Muḥammad, then a twenty-five-year-old merchant in the city of Shíráz, approached a traveler near the city gates. The traveler, Mullá Ḥusayn, had made it his life's mission to find the "Promised One," Who, according to scriptural prophecies, was believed to be in the world at that time.

The stranger invited Mullá Ḥusayn to his home, then startled him by answering his unspoken spiritual questions. Mullá Ḥusayn had found the person for whom he was looking.

Siyyid 'Alí-Muḥammad, who became known as the Báb, a title that means "gate," described His role as the door through which the universally anticipated revelation of God to all humanity would soon appear. A second Divine Messenger was to come Whose teachings would begin the age of peace and justice promised in all of the world's faiths.

The Báb claimed that recognition of this next Prophet would require "eyes of the spirit"—vision unclouded by personal attachments or preconceived notions. The promised Day of God, He declared, required new standards of conduct and a nobility of character that the Creator had destined for humanity, but which it had yet to achieve. "Purge your hearts of worldly desires," the Báb told His earliest followers, "and let angelic virtues be your adorning."[3]

The Báb described the anticipated divine teacher as "Him Whom God shall make manifest." Ḥusayn-'Alí, one of the earliest and most faithful followers of the Báb, would, in 1863, become known to history as Bahá'u'lláh, the Promised One Who was to begin a new world religion.

---

* "The Lord of the Age," one of the titles of the promised Qá'im [Islam's promised one].

In a society in which moral breakdown was rampant, the Báb's assertion that the spiritual renewal of society depended on "love and compassion" rather than "force and coercion" stirred enormous hope among all classes of people in Persia. His call for spiritual reformation—in particular, the uplifting of women and the poor, and the promotion of education for all—provoked an angry, fearful response from those who held religious and secular power in an oppressive society that had changed little since medieval times.

Persecution of the Bab's followers rapidly ensued, and thousands were killed in brutal massacres. The remarkable courage, even joy, that many of His followers exhibited in their commitment to their beliefs in the face of such violence was documented by a number of Western observers, including Leo Tolstoy. Eventually, the Báb was imprisoned and publicly executed before a crowd of ten thousand in 1850.

Over a century and a half later, the spirit of the Báb informs the lives of Bahá'ís, some five million of us, who see ourselves as citizens of one world and friends of all faiths.

A Day That Will Not Be Followed by Night

In a life beset by darkness, Bahá'u'lláh shed unfailing light.

The month of May holds two very significant holy days for members of the Bahá'í Faith. On May 23rd we commemorate the Declaration of the Báb, the landmark event in 1844 that saw the inception of a new faith that affirms the teachings of all the major world religions. On May 29th Bahá'ís observe the anniversary of the passing of the Faith's Prophet-Founder, Bahá'u'lláh.

Bahá'u'lláh's quiet exit from this world in 1892 stands in marked contrast to the nearly fifty years of imprisonment, exile, suffering, and torture that preceded it. It seems that no matter the upheaval and pain of His worldly days, the motivating purpose and power of His life and teachings embody the ultimate invitation we've all been given—to transcend this world in favor of a greater and deeper spiritual reality.

Born to nobility in nineteenth-century Iran, Bahá'u'lláh seemed destined for a life of ease. He chose instead to minister to those in need, which early in life earned Him the appellation "Father of the Poor."

When He first heard of the spiritually revolutionary teachings advanced by a young man known as the Báb, He immediately embraced them and sought to further their message of love and unity. This would cost Him everything He had and led to a life of continued exile and imprisonment due to His affiliation with this new faith that generated so much displeasure among Muslim clerics and others in power. This same new message of hope cost twenty thousand early followers their lives.

Bahá'u'lláh received the light of divine revelation in 1852 in one of the world's truly darkest places, an infamous Iranian prison known as the Black Pit. Imprisoned because of His religious beliefs, He was surrounded by scores of the very worst of criminals, burdened with two heavy chains, each weighing 150 pounds, that would leave scars on Him for the rest of His life.

Once He was finally freed, He was stripped of all His former wealth and property and exiled to Baghdad, the first of four banishments that He and His family would suffer. They would be sent to Constantinople, Adrianople, and ultimately to the stench-filled prison city of 'Akká in the Holy Land. Wherever He was sent at others' command, a curious interplay would continue to unfold— His enemies bent on His annihilation on the one hand, and, on the other hand, an increasing number of everyday citizens coming to love Him. Wherever He lived, His wisdom and radiant character would eventually earn the admiration of people from all walks of life. Fearful of this, the authorities kept sending Him farther into exile, hoping His influence would be extinguished.

In time, the writings of His revelation exceeded one hundred volumes and were addressed to believers and detractors, kings and commoners. For more than forty years He proclaimed a message of the coming-of-age of humankind in words such as these:

> It is incumbent upon all the peoples of the world to reconcile their differences, and, with perfect unity and peace, abide beneath the shadow of the Tree of His care and loving-kindness. It behooveth them to cleave to whatsoever will, in this Day, be conducive to the exaltation of their stations, and to the promotion of their best interests. . . . Soon will the present-day order be rolled up, and a new one spread out in its stead. Verily, thy Lord speaketh the truth, and is the Knower of things unseen.[4]

While He was technically still a prisoner of the state, Bahá'u'lláh died in the ancient city of 'Akká in a tranquil mansion surrounded by the countryside He had loved so much yet seen so little of in His life. Perhaps it's a testimony to the influence of the light He shed that the names of those who persecuted Him have been forgotten, yet less than 150 years later, more than five million people around the world—from every national, racial, ethnic, and religious background—remember Him. The religion He founded is among the fastest growing and is the second-most widespread in the world. And His teachings are being put into practice not only by Bahá'ís, but by humanity in general.

His whole aim, God's intended goal for humanity in this day, He once told a Western visitor, was "the good of the world and the happiness of the nations"[5]—the *happiness* of the nations. For this He endured the wrath and hatred of those who did not see their own interests advanced by His teachings.

Even in His final moments, deep in the heart of night as He lay dying, Bahá'u'lláh comforted those gathered around Him, emphasizing to them kindly, "I am well pleased with you all."[6]

"Jináb-i-Mírzá Ismá'íl, a believer present in that last audience with Bahá'u'lláh, has recorded: 'Tears flowed from my eyes and I was overcome with feelings of grief and sorrow after hearing these words. At this moment the Blessed Perfection bade me come close to Him, and I obeyed. Using a handkerchief which was in His hand, Bahá'u'lláh wiped the tears from my cheeks. As He did so, the words of Isaiah [25:8], ". . . and the Lord God will wipe away tears from off all faces . . .", involuntarily came to my mind.'"[7]

Thank You, 'Abdu'l-Bahá

Picture someone who consistently put others before himself and exuded remarkable happiness while doing so, and you have a rough idea of why so many loved 'Abdu'l-Bahá so much.

I think a lot about gratitude each November. Even back when I was making construction-paper turkeys by tracing my small hand and decorating its shape with feathers, I understood that that's what our major U.S. holiday—Thanksgiving—was for.

In recent years I've tended to reflect more on the relationship between gratitude and generosity—between thanks and giving. The examples of these that I've witnessed in many lives seem to suggest that the more you consciously cultivate one, the more you automatically intensify the other.

Nowhere has this been personified for me more thoroughly, and inspiringly, than in the life of someone who also comes to mind around the end of November, at least if you're a member of the Bahá'í Faith, as I am. November 26th and 28th are dates associated with events in the life of 'Abdu'l-Bahá, whose father, Bahá'u'lláh, was the Faith's Prophet-Founder.

Picture someone who consistently put others before himself and exuded remarkable happiness while doing so, and you have a rough idea of why so many loved 'Abdu'l-Bahá so much. From 1853 until 1910, from the time he was nine until his late sixties, he was more or less a prisoner together with the rest of his family. They were imprisoned because the things his father suggested about what would remedy mankind's ills never found much favor among those who held positions of power and authority. Perhaps that's because those who held that power didn't find their personal interests advanced by his teachings.

Stories about 'Abdu'l-Bahá play a key part in the life of Bahá'í families because he exemplified precisely what a life would look like when guided entirely by spiritually motivated choices. His actions illustrate the very qualities that his father urged humanity to explore, develop, and, perhaps most important of all, apply.

In raising our children, my husband and I found no better example to turn to when looking at questions of spiritual integrity. This was so much the case that the question we typically found ourselves asking in the face of many challenges was, "What would 'Abdu'l-Bahá do?"

Once he was finally free in 1910, he began a three-year journey through Europe and the United States. His goal was to impart the teachings that his father had brought to people across the world. 'Abdu'l-Bahá's spirit shone so brightly that even some who had declared themselves his enemies eventually arose to love and protect him.

One story about him remains my favorite because it illustrates both literally and symbolically just what sort of person he was. It occurred when he was probably about six years old, at a time when his family, who had descended from nobility, still had wealth. (A few years later that wealth would be seized by the government, and they would all become exiles.)

On the day in question 'Abdu'l-Bahá was sent out with an adult companion to inspect the work of the shepherds tending his father's sheep. When the inspection was finished and he turned to leave, the man who had accompanied him said, "It is your father's custom to leave a gift for each shepherd."

'Abdu'l-Bahá grew quiet for a while. He hadn't known or expected this and didn't have anything with him to give them. Then an idea came to him that made him very happy. He would give them the sheep!

When his father heard about this, He was, rather than angry or displeased, absolutely delighted with this early evidence of truly spontaneous generosity. He humorously remarked that everyone had better take good care of 'Abdu'l-Bahá, because someday he would give himself away.

And that is exactly what history shows that he did, over and over, all while bringing joy everywhere he went. Although I'm a long way from emulating that standard myself, I do know that gratitude and generosity are two prime factors in the equation. I hope that's at least some progress from the simple, self-motivated gratitude I felt back when I was tracing those turkey shapes. 'Abdu'l-Bahá's more encompassing kind of giving and gratitude can help heal a whole world.

CHAPTER 13

TAKE THOU THY PORTION

*"O wayfarer in the path of God! Take thou thy portion of the ocean
of His grace, and deprive not thyself of the things that lie hidden
in its depths. Be thou of them that have partaken of its treasures.
A dewdrop out of this ocean would, if shed upon all that are in
the heavens and on the earth, suffice to enrich them with the
bounty of God, the Almighty, the All-Knowing, the All-Wise.
With the hands of renunciation draw forth from its life-giving
waters, and sprinkle therewith all created things, that they may be
cleansed from all man-made limitations and may approach
the mighty seat of God, this hallowed and resplendent Spot."*

—Bahá'u'lláh, *Gleanings from the Writings of Bahá'u'lláh*

The Remedy Resides in Us

What, I wondered, was our life as a nation going to be like,
now that it had, like those four flight plans, taken
such an abrupt and terrible turn?

It's one of those life-changing moments you never forget. My father and I were on our last leg of a trip south from his summer place in Maine to his Florida home. As we drove, we reminisced about his years in Civil Defense after a twenty-two-year Army career, my mother's experience during the Blitz in England during World War II, and the incredible good that terrible times can often uncover in people.

Then, as we were passing through Atlanta, we spied an electronic message board over the interstate that read, "National Emergency—All Airports Closed."

As I turned on the car radio, information was instant and omnipresent. In the twenty minutes that we'd been out of touch with national news, there had been an awful, unfathomable cascade of events too large to even grasp. The dangling detail of the still unaccounted-for United Airlines flight 93 is what chilled me most. (Of course, I hadn't yet seen the images of New York's skyline.) I remember experiencing a feeling of smallness and vulnerability unlike any I could remember feeling before, as all my illusions of safety came down at once, like those two shattered towers.

This was my father's first return to the South since my mother's death ten months before. One thing I was grateful for was that he hadn't been alone on a day so terrible that it would come to be known worldwide simply by its date, 9/11.

What, I wondered, was our life as a nation going to be like, now that it had, like those four flight plans, taken such an abrupt and terrible turn? My first thought was, as my father and I had just been discussing, that such magnitude of terror and pain can often unleash a commensurately large outpouring of human goodness, the kind that seems to flood to the surface when things are almost too dreadful for us to bear. I hoped that larger numbers of us would deepen our resolve to cultivate that greater and higher part of us, the one that contributes to the most lasting, beneficial outcomes. And I hoped that this kind of response would last well beyond the weeks and months to come.

Four days later, after a category 3 hurricane had made landfall near my dad's Florida home and I'd truly begun to wonder whether the world was coming to an end, I took my place in a blocks-long line at Tampa International Airport. I was praying that this might really be the day that I'd be able to get home to New Hampshire. If I did, I'd be on one of the very first flights in the country that day, a day when many wished that we'd never have to fly again.

Every single child I saw that day looked scared. Most of the younger ones clutched their backpacks like stuffed animals, if they didn't happen to be holding those, too. Their parents looked grim, if not equally frightened.

Most everyone seemed to be holding it together, though, except for a boy of about nine, who, with his parents and younger brother, was waiting to board the same plane I was. His terror had simply become too large for him to contain. His plaintive sounds were agonizing, perhaps because so many of us were feeling exactly the same way but had suppressed our feelings way down deep inside. His poor parents, exhausted after days of canceled flights—a trip to Disney World that had become a nightmare from which they couldn't seem to awaken—were doing their best to calm him, with no effect.

Gradually, some of us waiting in the same terminal as this family stepped forward to try to reassure him. Obviously a polite child, he would leave off his agitation for a time and hear us out, but his sobs and desperation would soon return. He was convinced that if he got on this airplane, on any airplane, he was going to die.

The pilot and flight attendants took gentle, patient time with him yet gained little ground. The person who finally made the difference was a grandmotherly passenger with a soft Southern accent who takes that flight every other week for business travel. She introduced all of the flight crew to him by name as her friends, then asked him a question I didn't hear, but that he took a while to consider before answering. She told him it was OK if he felt afraid, and she told him that she'd felt that way, too.

Then I heard her say, "We need you to come with us, because it's important to be with your family and to go home. We need to be together, because we all have to help each other now. That's how we can stay safe, and how we can feel OK again."

When she put her arms around him, he relaxed against her as though relieved and stayed there for an unhurried while. When boarding began, he joined his family quietly. He suddenly remembered his bewildered younger brother and took cards out of his pocket so that they could play together.

I'm sure this wise and compassionate woman's words ultimately made sense to him. They definitely helped him realize that he wasn't alone in his fears. We were all scared, but we had to continue on with our lives because, indeed, we had important things to do, and we needed him to help us do them. That way, we could help each other feel better again.

She seemed to know exactly what we should say and do for our children—and each other. I don't think the essential wisdom in her response has changed very much at all, or that it applied only to that day, or to how we'd survive and go on after something like September 11th. But I do know that I need to be reminded of it every so often so that I won't forget.

Each Day a New Beginning

*Whatever our faith, or lack of it, and no matter how long
our personal winters may have been, the springtime of
divine grace always offers us another chance.*

I've been tracing a path of family history, following portions of the route that brought my parents together in England during World War II and eventually resulted in my speaking German almost as early as I spoke my mother tongue.

During the U.S. occupation of Europe after the war, my military family spent two tours in Germany, the second of which holds my oldest memories. When we sailed across the Atlantic to a very new life, military housing in Germany was at a premium, so we lived "on the economy," moving into a tiny village forty-five minutes from Frankfurt. There, a family named Geis welcomed us into the ground floor of their home while they squeezed upstairs to make room for us.

I say welcomed because, contrary to popular belief about German-American relations at the time, that's exactly how it feels in my memory. They were kind, generous, really, even though they had very little, particularly after the war. But while they no doubt also welcomed the money they were paid for sharing that clean, accommodating space, they always felt far more like hosts or friendly relatives than landlords to me.

What I remember most is how cheerful and happy they always were. I later learned that Herr Geis, the husband and father of the family, was, like my family, a recent arrival in Germany. Before that, his wife and children had waited fifteen long years while he was a prisoner of war in a Russian prison camp, wondering whether they'd ever see him again. I understand now that after he came home, they saw every day as a new beginning and treated it like something too precious to waste on anything but gratitude and joy.

It was during Easter week that the couple and I shared one of my earliest intercultural exchanges. One day my parents had some complicated appointments and errands, and the Geises offered to watch me while they were away. I was four and delighted in the prospect of spending the day with our hosts. My day involved little more than following along behind the couple as they did their chores. We prepared the field behind their home for planting, and they helped me find some stray potatoes they'd missed at harvest time.

After we'd eaten those potatoes at the midday meal, together with eggs we'd collected from their hens, they introduced me to my first Easter eggs.

We were coloring them when my parents appeared at their kitchen door, bearing some traditional American fare—Hershey's chocolate bars and a big bowl of popcorn—that they'd bought to celebrate Easter and to thank the Geises for their hospitality.

Most Germans had never seen popcorn since corn was grown only for animal feed in Europe in those days. That bowl lasted for hours as the Geises removed a piece at a time, holding it up and marveling as they named the creature or object that its shape approximated. Eventually, we all began to do the same amid lots of laughter. It ended up being quite a good vocabulary lesson for everyone and helped us to overcome our collective language barrier.

This event stands out in my memory because it signals such a perceptible shift in my family's bond with the Geises, the kind that meant they'd become regular guests at our on-base apartment long after we'd moved out of their home. Few other American families had this kind of friendship with their German hosts, and after my mother's horrific experiences during the Blitz in Britain, most anyone would have forgiven her if she'd been hesitant to embrace Germans. This experience, along with countless other memories of living in different places across the United States and abroad with my family, reminds me of how grateful I am that my parents always seemed able to see the humanity in any situation, above and beyond any history or politics.

A German friend recently shared a story with some very similar parallels to my family's stay with the Geises, yet his story is one that gives a glimpse into a German family's experience, too. Toward the very end of the war, on Good Friday, they expected their tiny village to be overrun at any moment by U.S. soldiers. The German troops were retreating, and my friend's family members, six adults and two children, were trying to decide whether they should stay put or hide in hills above the village.

In a previous war, their village had been wiped out in a similar situation, with every single person killed, so they were quite fearful. They also had a family member who was a prisoner of war overseas— one with whom they would later be reunited, and who would become my friend's father. Like the Geises, these folks were just trying to eke out their simple lives in terrible times, during a war that they wished had never happened.

They decided to stay in their home, and within hours, several vehicles pulled into their farmyard, and U.S. soldiers climbed out and ordered them upstairs while the soldiers took over the lower floor of the house. What my friend's aunt, who was among those present, most remembers is how young these soldiers looked to her at the time. As she and her sister peeked down from upstairs, she saw that the soldiers were having trouble figuring out how to light the cook stove, and so, to her family's horror, she bounded down to help them. (Her sister would later tease her that the only reason she'd done this was because those soldiers were so handsome.) That weekend, they all eventually feasted together on the farm's fresh eggs and the soldiers' rations in a shared meal around the kitchen table. On the morning of Easter Sunday, the family came downstairs to find the soldiers gone, along with a basket of hardboiled eggs that the family had colored earlier that week. In the basket's place was a huge stash of chocolate.

"My family hadn't seen chocolate for years," my friend said, "and this, combined with how carefully the soldiers had left everything in its place when my family had expected them to ransack the house, gave everyone great heart, and the possibility of believing that maybe things would be all right after all." The miracle of his father's return a short while later was the very best evidence of that, of course, and soon spring bulbs were blooming in the yard and, despite the ravages of the war, his family knew that they'd see green fields again.

It's no coincidence that the essence of Easter—resurrection—is about restoration and renewal. Whatever our faith, or lack of it, no matter how long our personal winters may have been, the springtime of divine grace always offers us another chance.

Even at Gunpoint

Imagine a commitment to justice and unity so strong that
even the prospect of death doesn't eclipse it.

I recently heard a speaker at a conference suggest that it's a spiritual imperative in life to have a personal mission statement. She further qualified that it needs to be "simple enough to be understood by a twelve-year-old," and it has to be "deliverable at gunpoint." Even in the most tumultuous or traumatic moments of our lives, it must be indelible enough that we never forget it.

It just so happens I know someone who managed to remember his mission statement at gunpoint. Or perhaps it's more accurate to say that being held up at gunpoint helped solidify what his mission was.

I've known Mark since he was twelve years old and have watched him grow up and weather quite gracefully the inevitable trials one encounters when he wants to fulfill his personal sense of mission through the arts, which is not made any easier when most everyone he knows is making it big in high tech or high finance.

When he was twenty-three, Mark and his roommate were returning home to their apartment after a late-night trip to the grocery store. They'd shopped on their way home from one of many long rehearsals of a production Mark was helping to direct at a nearby university. The play was called *Race*, an adaptation of a Studs Terkel book that addresses the issues of racism in America. It was perceived as a slightly controversial production in that, to enhance its themes, it segregated its audience into different sections for blacks and whites.

As the pair unpacked their groceries from the car, two black teenagers appeared and pointed handguns at the two white men. To his complete surprise, because of his immersion in the subject of race at the time, my young friend's first thought was not "Oh God, I am going to die" but "When this is over, how will I view black people?"

His roommate, obviously more focused on the first idea, dropped the bag of groceries he was holding, a response Mark thought unnecessarily wasteful, especially given how tight their resources were. The young muggers wanted the men's wallets. The roommate quickly complied, throwing his at their feet. Mark, according to his roommate's description, looked at them as if very, *very* disappointed and then slowly withdrew his wallet from his back pocket and held it out to them resignedly.

"Those muggers were kids, probably seventeen or eighteen—not professionals, but probably crack addicts, and they were scared. That's a dangerous finger to have on a trigger," Mark later noted.

The young muggers instructed the two men to run down the street and not turn around. Mark didn't know why they asked this, but he complied. His roommate was certain the assailants were going to shoot them in the back. It turned out they just wanted to run in the other direction. The two older men stopped after about thirty feet. They were alive. Their groceries were still there, if slightly the worse for wear.

They carried them inside and talked about what had just happened and ate Ben & Jerry's ice cream and laughed. It was an especially funny moment when Mark discovered he had a five-dollar bill in his shirt pocket, and then his roommate remembered that he had a twenty in his, a bill Mark had paid him back with earlier. The laughter helped lift the terrifying sense of fear they felt after what had just happened and reinforced their sense of gratitude for having lived through it.

The next day the tears and the shaking started to come, the inevitable kind that follow something like looking death in the face. But Mark connected with something even more important, he says.

"I realized that the work that I was doing to try and address and overcome the problem of racial prejudice was work that could eventually help eradicate the disparity that has created this type of situation my friend and I had faced. I was heading in the right direction, and this event only made it more real."

Even at gunpoint, the essence of his personal vision and mission somehow still loomed larger for my young friend than any fear the situation might have provoked. That's a mighty spiritual commitment indeed.

Thinning Yields Life's Choicest Fruits

Things add up, and while that can be a useful concept in the conservation of resources, it can sometimes dwarf our lives, and our time, when we don't make choices.

I chuckled the first time I noticed the empty gallon jug my husband had placed under a leaky faucet before we'd had time to repair it. That tap only dribbled about a drop every fifteen to twenty seconds. Yet when I needed cooking water a short time later, a full jug of that water was waiting nearby. Those drops had really added up, and it felt good to put them to use at least once before they went down the drain. Depending on what gets cooked in those pots, my husband sometimes even captures that water for double duty on flowerbeds or houseplants.

For years now, he has also brought home pounds of paper and cardboard from his workplace, where generating mountains of them is an occupational hazard. One or two evenings a week he takes an hour or two in front of the TV to sort, flatten, and bundle these up for recycling.

Initially, those quantities of waste paper looked pretty small. It was easy to think, why *bother*? Yet over time, as those resources were channeled toward reuse, they didn't simply disappear into dumpsters to later occupy space in our ever-growing landfills.

Watching even simple attempts at stewardship reminds me that many things, whether material goods or individual acts of human behavior, may not look like much in the moment, but they add up over time. And as we focus on being conscious about the decisions we make and how they affect the world around us, our life is enhanced. But if we run through our lives without stopping to reflect, our days can begin to feel choked off as a sea of activity—and stuff—begins to swallow us up.

When a friend gave me a batch of beautiful vegetables from her garden, I realized that there was one factor in their healthy growth that I'd never been savvy enough, or disciplined enough, to grasp. I had avoided thinning the plants in my garden, and, as a result, I'd had weaker plants and poorer yields. Since I hadn't practiced the discernment and choice that thinning requires, none of my plants had done very well.

Things add up, and while that can sometimes be a useful concept in the conservation of resources, it can dwarf our lives and our time when we don't make choices. The cultural suggestion that "you can have it all" produced a lot of folks like me who are struggling to learn how to thin our gardens—and our lives.

I had a rather timely epiphany about this a few months back when I visited a friend in Europe. I was surprised to see that as she made her to-do list, she customarily planned no more than half of her waking hours—two-thirds on the busiest days, which she keeps to a minimum.

When I asked why she didn't plan more, she said, "How else can I leave room for the unexpected, or spontaneity, or even the chance to change my mind?"

"But what about all the things you need to *do*?" I protested.

"Well, who *decides* that?" she asked, reasonably enough.

"Of course, this means that I have to say no to some things as well as yes to others," she qualified. "But I try to think of it as deciding what my yeses will be first, then seeing what time and room are left over after that."

By organizing her day through this disciplined budgeting of time, she gets the very most out of her "yeses," she said, and seldom feels as though she's doing something she doesn't want to.

Like that jug under our faucet, she's found the right design for recapturing a resource—her precious time—and using it in a useful and meaningful way rather than watching it drain away. Now *that's* my kind of stewardship.

CHAPTER 14

A MIRROR OF HIS OWN SELF

"Upon the inmost reality of each and every created thing He hath shed the light of one of His names, and made it a recipient of the glory of one of His attributes. Upon the reality of man, however, He hath focused the radiance of all of His names and attributes, and made it a mirror of His own Self. Alone of all created things man hath been singled out for so great a favor, so enduring a bounty."

—Bahá'u'lláh, *Gleanings from the Writings of Bahá'u'lláh*

The Legacy of a Happy Heart

Marian treated everyone like precious little mines of gems and maintained a happy, positive tone in this treasure hunt that simply left no room for negativity to make a nest.

There's a string of days in my memory that glimmer like pearls for me. They closed out the year when my friend Marian shared the last stage of her earthly life.

Although they occurred more than twenty years ago, they don't appear to be affected by time in any way. Those days shine as brightly and clearly in my mind as they did when they actually happened. In fact, in the intervening years, I've found that it's impossible to count all of the gifts those days have bestowed on me, as I continue to discover them.

It was faith that brought us together and that motivated every single aspect of our friendship. When we met, I was twenty and she was eighty, details that quickly seemed no more significant than the color of our eyes or the clothes we wore. From the first encounter, though the eyes of my own experience were very young, I could see that her ageless spirit had long ago found its way past the world's pain and confusion. How, I wondered, do you find a life like that?

She had become a willing, enthusiastic, and incredibly creative servant for the One Who had made her, and she was gifted at helping others feel the pure, uncomplicated, limitless effect of love. Her eyes—her whole face—shone with its transforming power.

More consistently than anyone I have met before or since, she demonstrated how much we barely recognize the potential that's been treasured in each of us, the reality that life grows better and better as we "unpack" this potential and also encourage and welcome it in others.

Marian taught me to trust that where souls truly meet and connect, an inseparable bond develops. Time and distance pose absolutely no barriers in that relationship. "And, Honey," she would say, "God loves us too much to want anything but the best for us, and the best

197

that we can possibly be. He knows the jewels He's treasured inside us, just waiting to be invited out."

Marian treated everyone like precious little mines of gems and maintained a happy, positive tone in this treasure hunt that simply left no room for negativity to make a nest. I'm so thankful that I had this reality reflected for me while I was so young, because it's given me more time to try to share it with others through my own aspiring efforts, whether as a spouse, parent, friend, or companion.

For the first two years that I knew her, I spent most every Tuesday evening in Marian's cozy living room. Then our paths diverged for a while, and we saw each other less. During those times, I'd often receive a call or letter in which she expressed ideas or addressed matters that were precisely what I had been struggling with—and usually hadn't told anyone else about. That mysterious power of love that she valued and encouraged others to value just seemed to keep leading to miraculous things.

I hadn't seen her for almost a year the day I first drove over to the small apartment she'd rented after her husband had passed away. When she met me at the door her face was the vivid gold that jaundice produces. I noticed that she talked animatedly about finishing all of the projects she was working on but said nothing about starting new ones.

Two weeks later, surgery revealed an inoperable tumor on her pancreas. For a few weeks, I made the fifty-mile trip to her house daily. The little things I did certainly weren't noteworthy at all; the radiance of her gratitude just made them seem that way.

She determinedly set about the projects she had yet to complete, wanting to be sure that others could carry on the work that had been so important to her throughout her life. She had developed a series of educational programs designed to help bring out the best in people's very highest nature. Like so much of her work, these efforts were aimed toward those whom society tends to overlook or forget.

During those days after her diagnosis, she seemed to thank God constantly for the mental clarity that enabled her to pursue her work in what were the last weeks of her life. "Prayer and the Word of God can be *mighty* powerful nourishment," she'd often say with a twinkle. Her soul, positively exhilarated about this next stage of her journey, was very patient with her physical self, nonetheless. I felt transported as I watched her and as we talked matter-of-factly about life and death.

One day, looking very small where she sat in an overstuffed chair, she leveled those brilliant eyes on me and said, "Honey, I don't think it will be long now. I can feel how much more tired I'm getting every day. But God has let me complete everything I hoped to do!"

Her joy enveloped me like arms in a wonderful embrace. Yet my drive home was tinged with sadness, because this, I knew, meant it was time to say good-bye.

Then I experienced something that made me willing to entrust even my sadness to God, young and unpracticed as I was in doing so. I was bringing Marian home from what would likely be her final doctor's appointment. Eating had become exceptionally difficult for her, and I knew she was downplaying what was surely considerable pain.

Then, to my surprise, she spotted a sign for homemade soup in a restaurant window and asked me to stop. When we did, we learned that the soup was long gone and the choices on the sticky menu were pretty meager. A handful of grim-looking people hunched silently over their plates as flies swarmed around the room. Could a place *be* more depressing? I wondered.

Marian's radiant face shone in the midst of it all like a beacon. She didn't eat much of what the harried-looking server put in front of her, but I swear that Marian was able to feed the waitress instead. Marian softly said a few things that suddenly made the waitress laugh and smile and appear quite beautiful. Then others began to talk a little, and soon there was laughter and happiness all around in what, just a little while before, had been a dreary, dingy place.

Marian's eyes sparkled like jewels, and I remembered something she'd often assert with a similar look in her eyes: "We continually overlook the power of love."

Neighbors and friends still tell the story of what they experienced in those hours in her home before Marian left this world a few days later. The room seemed to fill up with love and happiness, they say. They didn't want to leave.

She used to tell me that, at an earlier time in her life, being ungrateful and impatient had been two of her most difficult spiritual battles, something I often found impossible to imagine.

"Then, when I was ready to give up on this life, something suggested to me that it was time to stop my fighting, and I heard those words that Jesus promised: 'The Spirit of God is working in your midst.'"

From the day she accepted the "Spirit of God" and the teachings of the Bahá'í Faith that drew her closer to Him, she became an unfailing channel for its truth. I can still feel her love at work in my life today, and I feel my undying connection with her most strongly when I strive to do the same.

So Enduring a Bounty

Heaven forbid someone would flunk a course because I fumbled
a plastic baby or let it cry too long on my watch.

"I'm babysitting this morning, so why don't you come over here?" my
friend Chele said when I telephoned her one day.

It was the kind of quiet Saturday morning we don't often get to
share. She makes some of the best European-style coffee I've ever
had, and her company and conversation are even more satisfying and
flavorful. We became friends through our mutual love for children
and what we both feel really matters most, the spiritual aspect of all
of God's children, whatever their age.

The "baby" in question was actually her teenage daughter's charge,
"Catie," a life-size, anatomically correct doll that had come home
from school with her as part of a class assignment designed to help
young people gain up-close experience with the nonstop responsibility
of child care. Chele's daughter had to work that morning, so Chele, as
many grandparents do, had become the de facto babysitter.

Now, I knew about the eggs and plastic dolls that some high school
students bring home from similar classes. Students are required to
carry these with them at all times (or arrange care for them), and
obviously, the experience is bound to raise their consciousness about
the demands and responsibility required when an infant comes into
your life. But technology has really upped the ante in this experience
now. When I arrived at Chele's house, sitting beside her on the porch
in a plastic carrier was a lifelike doll dressed in pastels—lifelike
enough that I did a double-take when I first saw her.

Chele introduced her the way she would with any two people, and I
went through the motions of saying hello, though my brain registered
something like "plastic doll, object" and moved eagerly toward the
good coffee. As I took my first sips, however, it was obvious that
Chele's orientation toward this little bundle was considerably attuned.
Frankly, it put a bit of a damper on the lively conversation I'd been
looking forward to.

Having Catie here was surprisingly like having a real baby in the house, Chele told me. She'd even been cooing just minutes before I arrived. I did succumb to a rather insensitive thought at that point that Chele may have gone just a bit over the edge with all this.

Then little Catie started to cry. And cry.

The latest version of these "babies" comes equipped with what can only be described as stealth intelligence. In essence, they can go off like little alarms at any moment, which, of course, makes them lifelike indeed. A computer chip and motion sensor mean that this small companion needs (and internally monitors the intake of) regular physical nourishment. It registers whether you support its head and neck properly. It needs diaper changes (there are sensors there, too) and a short time after taking in that physical nourishment, it develops the need to burp. And sometimes, as with all of life's wild cards, its cry is simply something that you can't quiet with a preplanned solution of any kind.

That first time I heard Catie rev up, I felt something awaken in me at a very deep level, kind of like rediscovering body memory that knows how to perform a task you haven't attempted in years. This cry was real. A recording, to be sure, but so genuine-sounding (and increasingly louder) that no one with hearing could remain unaffected by it. Chele shifted and repositioned Catie in her arms about a half-dozen ways for what felt like fifteen minutes, but was probably only two. During this time, a neighbor actually stopped by on his way out and remarked, over the din, that he hadn't even known there was a baby in the house. Finally, Catie burped and quieted.

After this, she no longer seemed like a lump of plastic. My inner antennae had been activated, and I could still feel them twitching. In less than twenty minutes, two midlife women had become the hostages of a small plastic doll. We both chuckled at the realization.

Then Chele's husband called from where he was away on business travel, and Catie started up again. Chele changed the diaper whose color showed the need for replacement. But Catie kept crying, and Chele didn't have enough hands for the phone and Catie both. As I reached for Catie instinctively, I was automatically focused on handling a baby carefully. Heaven forbid someone would flunk a course because I fumbled a plastic baby or let it cry too long on my watch.

The same little rocking dance with which I paced with my own babies took over instantly, as did the soothing sounds, the molding of Catie's form against me, and the emotional space into which I shifted. I call it the "being with" energy. I think of it as finding a center I know is always there, then simply acting from that space while imagining a beautiful light coming down on me and whoever is in the vicinity. It's the only way I ever found to help a baby quiet. I have to be truthful and say that however much I love life and children, a baby's crying can be torture to the human nervous system. It calls for a kind of surrender that seems an inevitable portal to the way of prayer if you want to avoid hysteria yourself.

The fleeting recollection crossed my mind that this was a plastic doll I was holding. But it was still crying, and this was all I knew how to do, and I figured it could at least get the two of us through one phone call I knew Chele wasn't likely to drag out.

By the time she hung up, Catie was quiet. Chele expressed her marvel and complimented my auntie skills. I joked that the battery must have run down. Then I realized that what Catie's crying had evoked in me was an innate desire to communicate: "I see you, I hear you. You matter. I might not be able to make this better, but I'll stay with you." Fairly essential ingredients if you want to be able to relate to another person.

These were always a part of that "being with" energy, and ultimately they were a gift for both me and the child, as they unfailingly brought us a sense of oneness and togetherness. The peace of that feeling wasn't from us directly, but *through* us, somehow. It always seemed to help each of us access that quiet, safe place that's waiting for us, the one that seems to hold us at all times, whether we know it or not.

Babies and children help adults remember and reach for that place that gives us a feeling of safety and comfort, as long as we know and trust that it's there in the first place. Most of life's hardest tests invite us toward the same thing, learning and working toward reconnecting to that sense of calmness that's all-embracing as soon as we turn toward it. It's the required surrender that often trips us up along the way.

"Dost thou reckon thyself only a puny form when within thee the universe is folded?"[1] Bahá'u'lláh reminds us in the Seven Valleys. There's a whole lot of light, both within us and all around us, just waiting to meet us when we turn toward it.

Little Angel, Big Prayer

God is near, astonishingly near to us.

When I heard my father's voice on our answering machine, I knew instantly why he was calling. He was far too deaf to use a phone anymore. It had to mean that my mother had died.

It was a shock so sudden and huge that it seemed to pull everything into a silent vacuum along with it. This was a woman whose energy and love had touched so many lives in an intimate way that her absence seemed almost unthinkable.

The demands of organizing the funeral pushed us through the next days, held up by a chain of prayers uttered by family and friends all over the world. Her recent illness meant that, despite the pain of our loss, this really was her Lord's reprieve. My sister and I both felt this, which made her feel very close to us.

But my father seemed encased in a mountain of ice, moving through the hours in sad-faced silence. Her near-constant companion for sixty years, he couldn't visualize life without her and didn't seem to want to try.

I was relieved when he accepted my offer to stay on with him for a week after everyone else left. But eventually I had to return home, too. He lasted six days on his own and then collapsed. My sister brought him back to her new home, midway between his Florida one and mine in New Hampshire. He was admitted to a nearby hospital for surgery, and for the second time in three weeks I boarded a plane on short notice.

I was appalled when I saw him. My sister and I knew that, regardless of his illness, he was really fighting to find the will to live—and might not succeed. My prayers begged God to sustain him, help him feel God's love, as well as ours. But as Dad became increasingly unresponsive, my heart sank more heavily than ever.

On Christmas Eve I asked God to help me do what I could, surrender to him what I couldn't, and trust that He held Dad in His loving hand, whatever the outcome.

I had to make myself go to the hospital the next morning. I was astonished to find Dad sitting up. Though he'd been immobile in bed for nearly two weeks, he had taken not one, but two walks that morning, the nurse told me.

His eyes were very bright when I arrived. "Hon, I've got to get out of here," he said. "Your mother sent a little angel last night, who told me that's what God wants me to do—get up, and go on with my life."

As if to test his sincerity, circumstances prevented him from being discharged on the holiday, which meant I had a chance to learn more about that "little angel" when a friend called to wish me a happy Christmas.

A treasured prayer companion, she has an admirable godmother's relationship with her five-year-old nephew. She takes her duty to champion his spiritual life very seriously, and they talk together about God all the time.

"Tristan was here Sunday," she told me. "We found a scraggly branch, stuck it in the snow, and made a Charlie-Brown Christmas tree. When we were decorating it, he looked at me and asked, 'Auntie Di, are you OK?'"

"I told him I've been worried about my friend because her mommy died and her daddy's been so sad that nobody knows what to do."

She described how the little boy paused for a moment, then said, "Well, of COURSE the daddy's sad. The MOMMY died!"

His clear child's wisdom brought sudden tears to my eyes as I listened.

Then she shared his next words. "But God can make anything better, right, Auntie Di? Tomorrow's special because it's Jesus's birthday. I'm going to ask God to tell the daddy that the mommy is with Jesus and that everything is going to be OK."

There was a long, teary silence on my end as she finished.

On Christmas Eve, that little boy had offered his faith-filled, *confident* prayer. That Christmas was a turning point for my dad— and I am sure it is due entirely to the power of prayer. He would remember it always as the season when, warmed by the Light of the World, and touched by a little angel, he found the will to live.

That healing benefited father and daughter alike. Out of the depths of my own distress, I was lovingly reminded once again that "unless you change and become like little children, you will never enter the kingdom of heaven" (Matthew 18:3).

Join the Circle: Reflect on the Life of the Spirit

*True friendships have absolutely nothing to do with life's
outer appearances and everything to do with that inner
light that glimmers in each of us.*

As summer shifts into autumn each year, I instinctively begin the necessary hunkering in that precedes New England winters. I begin to retreat into my nest and stay at home a little more often, and I also tend to spend more time reflecting on where the year has brought me this far.

As I draw my attention closer to home in this personal spiritual harvest, I grow more conscious of the neighborly small-town life I'm blessed to have. When I lived in China's second largest city for just four short months, I certainly experienced some of the most exciting days of my life, but I also, in my inevitable culture shock, encountered a yearning for my hometown stronger than any I'd ever known.

While that town's no longer the kind where I'd leave my car running when I pop into a store, it's still the sort of place where you can dial a wrong number and end up having an awfully nice chat with whoever's on the other end. The bonds you form in a place like this are true friendships that have absolutely nothing to do with life's outer appearances and everything to do with that inner light that glimmers in each of us. They are spiritual connections, as important to life and survival as clean air and water.

I saw how hungry people are for these things recently when I was in a small nearby city. My husband and I were having dinner with friends at a sidewalk café when an endless parade of fire engines began screaming past. After the first ten minutes, the trucks began to show the names of various surrounding towns, and we thought, *is the world coming to an end? What has happened?* The sense of urgency alone had a galvanizing effect that began to draw people's attention together, as such developments often do.

The fire, it turns out, was at a house right around the corner, tucked down a narrow drive behind other houses, which made it very difficult for the fire engines to reach. The neighborhood's crooked little side streets were filled with onlookers. People weren't ogling so much as watching the fire-fighters' systematic efforts with admiration and support. They brought them drinks and cheered them on, or comforted the family who, with all their pets, had at least gotten out of the inferno safely.

As I looked around, it seemed that everybody was engaged in conversation with someone else. Contrary to the norm, nobody was in a hurry to rush off to something. And every single one of those dozens of people was hands-free of any electronic personal device. Some of those conversations were still going on long after the last truck drove away. It was as though, in the midst of all that smoke and heat, we'd all found a spring of connection and association we'd been thirsting for.

"The fundamental purpose animating the Faith of God and His Religion is to safeguard the interests and promote the unity of the human race, and to foster the spirit of love and fellowship amongst men,"[2] Bahá'u'lláh wrote.

The unity of the human race is a tall order, of course, but a spirit of love and fellowship is something we can each play a part in advancing on the local and neighborhood level.

This is just what Bahá'ís around the world are endeavoring to do. They're inviting their friends, neighbors, coworkers, and family members to sit together face-to-face and take that first step in building ties of fellowship, and getting to know each other on a deeply personal and spiritual level. They're reflecting together on life, in particular, the life of the spirit, the one from which love and fellowship tend to flow.

They're also seeking to help fortify each other's spiritual foundation and identity in an increasingly material world and to support each other to act on their God-given talents and capacities. No matter what the participants' religious background, or lack of it, they're experiencing the unifying spirit of collective worship and study and are pondering together such big questions as: What is life's purpose? What is the nature of the soul and how does it progress? What is the significance and effect of our deeds?

These groups are called Ruhi study circles and can be found taking place around the world. The circle is wide and welcomes anyone seeking spiritual nourishment. If you'd like to find a Bahá'í study circle near you, visit www.bahai.us/bahai-study-circles or call 1-800-22-UNITE.

CHAPTER 15

THE EARTH IS BUT ONE COUNTRY

"We cannot segregate the human heart from the environment outside us and say that once one of these is reformed everything will be improved. Man is organic with the world. His inner life moulds the environment and is itself also deeply affected by it. The one acts upon the other and every abiding change in the life of man is the result of these mutual reactions."

—Written on behalf of Shoghi Effendi,
The Compilation of Compilations, Vol. 1

Stewardship and Storage Lockers

As landscapes start to overflow with storage lockers,
our consuming culture now makes money housing the
disparity between our needs and wants.

In our neighborhood, spring and fall are each heralded by collections of household items and other goods that appear outside homes overnight in anticipation of the big seasonal trash pickup.

One morning years ago, I awoke to the clanging of aluminum tubing striking a metal surface. We'd left a cache of it outside the night before, stuffed into a trash barrel like unruly stalks of celery. The tubing was one of dozens of items we'd hauled to the curb from the dark recesses of our basement.

Outside, one man was methodically examining the goods we'd stockpiled while another was making the clanging sound as he tossed those tubes into a well-used pickup. Seeing these early birds find something they could use among our junk was a real jumpstart to my day.

All over town that week, people started to visit these roadside stashes to have a look. Nobody seemed self-conscious about it, and some were downright helpful. One woman pointed out a nice little cabinet she was giving away that's been a part of our kitchen ever since.

Nobody organized this "road mart" activity. The exchange just seemed to spring up by itself, almost as if we'd all been waiting for the opportunity.

As the piles grew, I discovered one morning that our rapidly growing prepubescent son no longer fit into his only white shirt, the one we'd bought just two months before, and the required attire for his school concerts. My wallet yawned empty when I looked inside.

Desperate, I phoned a fourteen-year-old friend of the family for help.

"Sure," he said, searching his closet. "I've got three—one should fit. And would you be willing to drive me downtown? My friend says there's some really good stuff out now, and we'd like to check it out."

The neighborhood where I dropped him off had a pile at every house. He looked delirious as he raced away, but not before I thanked

213

him for saving me—and my wallet—a trip to the store. This was my kind of grassroots economy, for sure.

Where our son was sometimes careless with new clothes, he treated this borrowed shirt like some sort of grail. "Better not spill on Seth's shirt," he said, tucking a napkin in his neck at dinnertime (a level of concern he'd never demonstrated with any of his clothes before). As we drove to the concert, he realized, "Hey, Mom! You didn't even *have* to spend money to get this shirt! I bet there are lots of ways not to spend money." I actively encouraged a new hobby of seeing how many alternatives to buying new things he could find.

Indeed, God, Who counsels that every hair of our heads is accounted for, urges stewardship of all things, including material goods. Worldly things benefit us most when we acquire and use them thoughtfully, so that they don't "own" us.

If ever we needed such stewardship, it's now. In one month, two friends described storage lockers from which they've never reclaimed goods after moving, because they haven't the space for (i.e., don't really need) them. I recently noticed several failed strip malls advertising space for personal storage. Where it once sold us the goods, our consuming culture now capitalizes on providing space for what we no longer need—or perhaps never needed in the first place. It's amazing that, even sitting forgotten and unused, those goods are still consuming energy.

The disparity between our genuine needs and our often undisciplined wants affects a wider sphere than that of our own lives, of course. For a long time it seemed possible to overlook this truth, but it stares back at us from every direction now. The more we acquire, the less we recycle or reuse, and the more energy we consume, the larger the "carbon footprint" we leave behind. No matter who's doing the studies about our impact on the environment, the evidence seems to indicate that it's those of us living in the United States who are leaving the biggest footprint.

In addition to conserving energy and preserving our shared home, knowing what we truly need and when we no longer need it is a valuable skill of discernment for many reasons, especially when it's matched with a spirit of generosity. Even if we have to spend the next couple of decades shifting our thinking and behavior in this way, wouldn't it be worth it if, as a result, we see the extremes of want and poverty—and of drowning in excess—disappear?

Some cultures have long held simple but effective solutions for renewing, recycling, and conserving resources in this way. A friend described one example of creative stewardship she witnessed on a visit with the Cowichan band of Native people in British Columbia. They introduced her to a long-established tradition called a potlatch, an event where participants bring belongings they wish to share or no longer need so that others will have access to them. She described a convivial affair with lots of music and food, and those of all ages going home with useful things, with few having to cart many old belongings home.

They don't have curbside trash pickup. But they do get together like this every once in a while to enjoy each other's company and pool resources.

Sounds like mighty good stewardship to me.

Green Is a Part of Everyone's Rainbow

*The real answers come not through anybody's political rhetoric
or promises, but through commitment manifested
person by person—and one neighborhood at a time.*

It was interesting to note the response I received when people heard that I was planning to attend a Green Movement Forum hosted recently by the Seacoast African American Cultural Center, one of my favorite local non-profits.

"Why does there need to be special focus on environmental issues and black people?" one person asked. "Don't environmental issues affect us all?"

Speaking broadly, that's true. But some happen to be living a little closer to the action these days.

The forum's conversation was less about the catastrophic threats of earth and climate change than it was about what many Americans are dealing with right now, environmentally speaking—living in places and conditions that undermine or even destroy their health. It was also about the remarkably effective possibilities created when regular folks simply respond to the needs they see around them and accompany others to do the same.

In Zena Nelson's neighborhood, it's hard to find good food, the kind that actually helps people stay healthy. The grocery store that most people's economic circumstances allow them to patronize has a produce section that rarely sees truly fresh fruit or vegetables. Most of what you find there is long past its prime. Living in the South Bronx as she does, she knows that most of her neighbors can't go all the way uptown or into Manhattan to obtain fresh produce, nor are they able to afford it, let alone buy organic.

So she took a clipboard and went door-to-door and talked to folks. She understands that the first step in wanting to help is to talk with those most affected by a problem and to listen well. And preferably to do this at the neighborhood level, since that's where any action we take is likely to have the most impact. Beyond that scale, prospects appear too overwhelming and people begin to beat a retreat.

Through creative thinking and consulting with others, Zena helped bring the South Bronx Food Cooperative to her neighborhood. This "green-shopping alternative" empowers local residents to buy nutritious food for less, to know where their food is coming from and how it's grown, to learn in adult and children's classes how to prepare different foods, and to find access to health screenings, nutrition workshops, and potentially valuable job skills.

Today this innovative solution has gained the support and involvement of New York's Montefiore Medical Centers, who are eager to track improvements in a neighborhood with a history of high mortality rates from diseases like diabetes and high blood pressure.

This endeavor has also accomplished something else, beyond helping people begin to eat better and guard their health. It has helped those living in Zena's neighborhood to learn more about working together and to really get to know each other. "What surprised us most," said Zena, "was the way this gave people a chance to use skills many others didn't even know they had," whether they were sixteen, as the co-op's storefront manager is, or great-grandparents. Among Zena's own contributions is getting up to meet the growers who come into the city to market their produce at 3 a.m.

If her neighborhood was steeped in health hazards, Rodney Stotts' is downright deadly. For anyone expecting government to provide the solution to our most enduring problems, Rodney's neighborhood is one indicator that it's in no hurry to do so, or to start especially "close to home."

In the shadow of the U.S. Capitol, Rodney's Anacostia neighborhood, as one news commentator put it, "might as well be on the far side of the moon for all official Washington cares." For decades its residents have eked out survival amidst some of the nation's worst poverty, crime, and violence. It's a place infiltrated by toxic waste (as one might imagine, cancer rates here are predictably off the charts). The river it's named for is so clogged with filth that the water itself has been masked by trash heaps one hundred feet high. And a seriously outdated sewage system has added human waste to that mix.

It's the kind of urban neighborhood where they always put the factories and the freeways, Rodney notes. The kind where, when you're young and find a way to survive, you're an endangered species.

Now the subject of several television documentaries, Anacostia began to change when a few committed people began to treat it like a neighborhood, and each other like neighbors. Rodney was making good money dealing drugs, though he says his days weren't exactly spent on what you'd call quality time. One day the look in his toddler's eyes changed something in his heart, and a short while later a friend connected him to the Earth Conservation Corps (ECC).

At first it was tough getting by on just a hundred dollars a week, but in time the value in the very hard cleanup work he'd signed up for began to mean more than almost anything ever had. In the past twenty years, the ECC has "graduated" more than 400 formerly at-risk young people from its development programs while also helping tens of thousands of local residents learn more about the land and water that are a part of all their lives. Members devote 1,700 hours to cleaning up the environment, protecting endangered wildlife, and providing community service to their neighbors and peers. This earns Corps members a stipend, health insurance, and child care benefits, as well as a $5,000 scholarship.

Recruiting young men and women from this inner-city community even if they have criminal records or are dropouts, ECC puts them to work in the incredibly demanding task of cleanup. The experience is similar to a boot camp that hones their commitment and their character. Then it leads them into increasingly more inspiring opportunities. One of Rodney's projects was participating in the successful reintroduction of the national symbol, the bald eagle, to a habitat that is, appropriately enough, near the nation's capital. He's stuck around ever since and has become the ECC's youth program coordinator.

The real answers to many of our most intractable problems appear to come not through anybody's political rhetoric or promises, but through commitment manifested person by person and one neighborhood at a time. In fact, as we survey the places in our country where true progress is taking place, it is neighborhoods that are at the forefront.

What does this have to do with me, we might ask? Well, in social-justice terms, it seems that environmental concerns, like health concerns, follow the pattern of how the body itself behaves. We know what the failure of one organ or system can mean to the others. Similarly, when it comes to the quality of human life in our world, things are inextricably interrelated, no matter what our presumptions and acquired knowledge may persist in trying to tell us. No matter where we happen to live.

Every backyard is somebody's, and usually that of somebody's children, too. And, as blood supplies and disaster relief so often remind us these days, those somebodies might turn out to be people I'll someday be glad to have in my world, whether I ever actually meet them or not.

True Spirit of Giving Brings Many Happy Returns

*What a grace when life allows our giving to be the
precise answer to someone's need.*

As members of the Bahá'í Faith, my family and I share a gift-giving season in late February, way past the time when holiday shoppers are cramming the malls for last-minute gifts. Yet we also appreciate sharing Christmas with our extended family and friends.

Last year one family we know was sitting around their Thanksgiving table when the subject of Christmas inevitably came up. Only this time, the discussion led to a little revolution.

"It all feels like it belongs to the stores and the advertisers more than anything else," said one. All agreed that, in their efforts to be good stewards, they felt frustration at how such a holy season had become focused on consumption of goods rather than celebration of spirit.

As Christmas approached each year, most of them found themselves in the midst of a sea of frenzied humanity, cramming holiday shopping, which had come to feel like an obligatory burden, into already over-scheduled days.

As their discussion lasted long beyond the coffee and pie, they decided to try an experiment. Why not find a different approach and actually enjoy this beautiful season completely and for all the right reasons?

What they devised together turned into one of the very best experiences they've shared. First, they took the holiday meal-planning off anyone's shoulders by making it a cooperative affair that three family members volunteered to oversee and organize. They'd already been leaning in this direction over the years, trying to find creative ways to keep any of them from getting marooned in the kitchen.

Their new gift-giving strategy was their biggest brainstorm. They agreed that whatever presents each chose to give, the gift had to involve recycling something that had already been owned or used. The focus wasn't about off-loading junk or unwanted items, but rather to find a way to personalize Christmas by really giving time and thought to finding something right for the recipient. The goal was to also reinvest an item with more meaning as it found a new life of usefulness for someone else.

Some resorted to visiting secondhand stores; some looked among their own belongings. One segment of the family had a little "trading day" with others they knew in order to create a cache of prospective items from which to choose. Some traded or bartered goods or services with others to obtain the right gift, and some made the gifts themselves.

One resourceful member created a wallet-sized, fabric-swatch booklet for a color-blind sibling, with colors clearly labeled so that if he ever chooses a purple shirt again when he thinks it's blue, he'll at least know how others identify that shade.

A grandchild who annually gobbled most of a certain cookie baked by his aunt received a tin canister of these. The tin, which was discovered at a church rummage sale, was shaped like his favorite Sesame Street character.

One much-appreciated gift was the photograph albums that several members made their pet project, assembled and captioned from photos they had on hand or from forgotten photos in drawers, closets, or boxes.

One environmentally friendly rule was that no commercial gift wrap was allowed. Most wrapped their gifts in newspaper, while some created their own hand-decorated paper or wrapped their present in a collage of magazine images inspired by the recipient. Other givers borrowed from a tradition associated with Saint Nicholas Day, celebrated on December 6th in Europe, in which the goal is to make the packaging or wrapping itself as creative or fun as possible. Since one recipient loved to play pool, the giver designed her package to look like a miniature pool table. Another family member had to wade through a dish of dark Jell-O to find his gift.

Beyond the money they saved, the credit-card balances they didn't run up, and the traffic and stress they avoided, this family found many different benefits that Christmas. Most said that they had actually looked forward to the day together and experienced a fun kind of anticipation that made them feel like kids again.

The best part, they say, is that the process of giving gifts in this way often became a source of wonderfully humorous or moving stories, which made their holiday together even more intimate and enjoyable. Those stories were almost gifts in themselves, gifts they're likely to share with each other over and over as holidays roll around each year.

When gift-giving is about people, it captures the deepest spirit of the season.

Not long after I heard about their experience, life gave me a precious little "pass it on with love" experience of my own. One of the very last things I bought for my father before he died was a small artificial Christmas tree. He was struggling to make peace with having to leave his home and accept the care of assisted living as he entered his final days at this time last year. And I was trying to create Christmas around him—while my heart seemed to be simultaneously breaking in half.

My daughter accompanied me to find this tree for her grandfather's new home, and we bought the very last one the store had. It was about the same height as my daughter's petite frame, with twinkling tiny lights already attached.

After my father died last June, that tree and the box it came in got stockpiled along with many other things I wasn't ready to face quite yet. Finally, a few weeks ago, I knew that it was time to pack it up along with a number of other things I needed to bring to the thrift shop. But it was very, very hard to think about taking it there.

"Let's set it up in its stand so that people are more likely to notice it and also see how very nice it looks," my husband suggested, then thoughtfully unpacked and assembled it.

The following day I drove a car packed to the gunwales to the local secondhand thrift store, feeling the weight of the grief and sadness that had been stirred by sorting through so many of my father's things.

Then as I was unpacking the tree from my car, they magically appeared—a kind-faced young man with his little girl clutching his hand. They came up to me tentatively and asked very politely whether, if I were going to leave the tree there anyway, it might be OK for them to take it.

Could my father, the universe, the Creator of it all—take your pick—have possibly sent a more profound and relevant form of reassurance?

I hugged them both spontaneously and said that, of course, I knew it would delight my father if they were to have it, and I hoped that they were going to have an absolutely wonderful Christmas.

Then I noticed the woman who was with them, too, standing off to the side. Just when I was thinking that they all must think I'm crazy, she gave me a big smile and thanked me, and then the other two, who were still a little stunned by my response, began lots of thanks-yous, as well. Her smile reminded me a little bit of my mother, I have to say.

In the Hidden Words, Bahá'u'lláh says of God's design, "To give and to be generous are attributes of Mine."[1] What a grace it is to us when life allows our giving to be the precise answer to someone's need.

Survival Is a Low-Bar Goal

*Wouldn't it make sense that our Creator has already supplied us with
the resources and strategies we require to flourish as one family?*

An online survey I stumbled upon invited response to a question
posed by theoretical physicist Stephen Hawking:

How can the human race survive the next hundred years?

"I don't know the answer," Hawking admits in a video clip posted
with the question. "That is why I ask the question, to get people to
think about it and to be aware of the dangers we now face."

Before the 1940s, the main threat to human life came from asteroid
collisions with Earth, collisions that had caused mass extinctions in
the past, he notes. "But the last of these was 70 million years ago, so
the likelihood that we will need the services of Bruce Willis in the
next hundred years is very small," Hawking quips.

I couldn't resist adding my own thoughts to the pages and pages
of very mixed responses posted on the Yahoo Answers Web site. At
this time in human history when this question often appears to be
closing around us more like a vise, I share these here respectfully
simply as food for thought:

Thanks, Dr. Hawking, for such an important question.

It occurs to me that many of the missing pieces in its answer might
include some basic antidotes to the effects of widespread materialism,
effects that can be found but are generally overlooked in cultures
throughout the world. It could be reinforced by the cultivation of a
worldview that affirms the essential nobility of humans as spiritual
beings. What if we try:

• encouraging cooperation between science and religion, viewing
  them more as complementary partners than adversaries. Maybe

224

issues such as climate change and global warming require just this sort of informed partnership;

- committing to the search for truth and principle in the solution of any problem, beyond clinging to established tradition or simple blind imitation of the past;

- welcoming more leadership from women, which could also lead to actual gender equality and collaboration. Leadership by others who have thus far been absent from positions of influence, and have also dealt with challenging issues in the very trenches of life, might bring with it new ideas and beneficial changes;

- developing societies and communities that are child-development-centered and truly child-safe—ones that treasure and support all families and offer the resources they need to carry out their highest potential, to draw out what is highest and best in all human beings;

- genuine regard and care for elders—treasuring them as a source of knowledge and respecting them as an invaluable resource in problem-solving;

- universal education for everyone founded on intellectual and spiritual understanding of the essential oneness of the human race and the development of the kind of individual inner character that leads people to prefer their neighbors before themselves. Also, cultivating through that education an eagerness to be of service and to solve problems;

- a willingness to forgo nationalism in favor of a sane patriotism and identification as part of a world culture;

- a consultative approach to decision-making and problem-solving both in the home and in the world;

- a willingness to recognize and be informed by the overwhelming similarities in revealed religious truth rather than emphasizing the far more minimal differences. Understanding why the differences exist in the first place;

- giving priority to cultivating the kind of innate spiritual nobility within each individual that is capable of recognizing that the honor of one is the honor of all. We've strayed quite some distance from this, but it's always present here to welcome us back.

As one great thinker once put it, why not try these things? We can always go back to the way things are if they don't make a difference.

Sincerely, and with thanks,
Phyllis Ring, Exeter, New Hampshire, U.S.

Weather or Not

If weather patterns around us seem unprecedented, what's being asked of us as one human family is even more so.

In January I expect to hear many sounds in my New Hampshire neighborhood, including scraping shovels and plows. But not once in fifty winters had I heard a lawnmower.

"I just couldn't stand seeing the grass growing even after we'd taken down the Christmas decorations," my neighbor explained. That same day, a friend in Seattle described unaccustomed snow, Texas relatives were immobilized by roads made impassable by an ice storm, and kids in shorts and tank tops were playing Frisbee on the lawn across the street.

A few days later the grass and confused bulbs and daylilies all along our street were flash-frozen in icy place, reminiscent of those images of Mount Vesuvius's victims in Pompeii and Herculaneum. And a besieged Northern Europe was cleaning up after . . . a *hurricane?* In *January?*

Among teasers for the evening news, one still asked, "Is global warming a reality?" The larger question really seems to be, why in the world are we still questioning and debating this? Here we stand at a juncture where unparalleled technological advances have contracted our world into a virtual neighborhood. We're instantly confronted not only with the pattern of every weather system across the planet, but also with scores of interrelated problems that threaten the world on which our survival depends. Yet headlines still seem more taken up with reality TV than with reality.

More than ever, the resolution of crushing poverty and oppression; intractable political, religious, and ethnic conflicts; and, perhaps most essential to our very survival, disruption of global ecosystems is calling for levels of cooperation and coordination that surpass anything in humanity's collective experience. It becomes more obvious by the day that the solutions to the kinds of challenges we face now can't be met without the involvement of representatives from all segments of the human family and all departments of human life—political, social, scientific, economic, and religious.

In fact, more than likely, it's only through the interaction of people from all cultures, races, and socioeconomic and educational backgrounds that creative approaches to sustainable development will be found at all. Plus, this kind of interaction is no doubt the only route to overcoming all of those lingering prejudices, misconceptions, and suspicions that currently dominate so many human relationships.

While it's essential that we recognize the interdependence between human life and our planet's environment, it seems that to really solve the world's problems, we need a deeper understanding of humanity's spiritual reality, the one that lies at the very essence of every single one of us. It's that spiritual nature of ours that's the source of the very qualities that engender unity and harmony, lead to insight and understanding, and make collaborative undertakings possible at all. Such qualities—compassion, forbearance, trustworthiness, courage, humility, cooperation, and willingness to sacrifice for the common good—are the "raw materials" needed for the very solution of the problems themselves.

As we consider the connection between the spiritual dimension of human existence and sustainable development in our world, we're being called upon to apply spiritual qualities and solutions to the material problems that humanity has created. If weather patterns around us seem unprecedented, what's being asked of us as one human family is even more so.

Just as individual human beings advance toward maturity by moving through a series of increasingly challenging tasks, so is humanity as a whole called upon to apply spiritual qualities to the challenges that the world faces in order to advance humanity's spiritual maturity. To attain such maturity, our understanding of spirituality must now embrace not only personal development and growth but also the collective progress of humanity as a whole.

In a nineteenth-century appeal to humankind to accept the central truth of its oneness, Bahá'u'lláh urged, "Regard ye not one another as strangers. Ye are the fruits of one tree, and the leaves of one branch. . . . The earth is but one country and mankind its citizens."[2]

While recognizing humanity's oneness implies a reawakening of the spirit of goodwill, it also suggests the need for something more far-reaching: a universal ethical imperative that, while touching the human spirit, also empowers every member of the human race to assume responsibility for the fate of our shared home. Without this, the peoples of the world are unlikely to become active, constructive participants in the global process of sustainable development, and we'll thus lack the enormous financial, technical, human, and moral resources necessary to achieve it.

World citizenship's time has truly come. If we have any doubt about that, we need only watch the weather.

For years there was a poster in our kitchen that showed a mother cradling an infant whose attention was trained on the toy ball his mother held, which resembled a miniature Earth. Above this scene were the words "Children ask the world of us."

Now, more encompassing wisdom seems to suggest that the world, and its Creator, are asking for the very best that all of its children have to give.

NOTES

INTRODUCTION

1. The Universal House of Justice, *Messages from the Universal House of Justice 1963–1986*, no. 151.5.
2. Ibid., no. 151.6.
3. 'Abdu'l-Bahá, *Star of the West*, vol. 7, no. 13, pp. 117–18.
4. 'Abdu'l-Bahá, *Selections from the Writings of 'Abdu'l-Bahá*, no. 23.7.
5. Bahá'u'lláh, The Hidden Words, Persian, no. 12.
6. 'Abdu'l-Bahá, *Paris Talks*, no. 53.5.

CHAPTER 1

1. Mother Teresa, http://quotationsbook.com/quote/21979.
2. Bahá'u'lláh, *Gleanings*, no. 130.1.

CHAPTER 2

1. Bahá'u'lláh, *Tablets of Bahá'u'lláh*, p. 127.
2. Bahá'u'lláh, *Epistle to the Son of the Wolf*, p. 93.
3. Gibran, *The Prophet*, p. 101.

CHAPTER 3

1. Bahá'u'lláh, *Gleanings*, no. 153.5
2. The Báb, *Bahá'í Prayers*, p. 226.
3. 'Abdu'l-Bahá, *Selections from the Writings of 'Abdu'l-Bahá*, no. 35.2.
4. Bahá'u'lláh, *The Seven Valleys and The Four Valleys*, p. 22.

CHAPTER 4

1. Bahá'u'lláh, The Hidden Words, Arabic, no. 32.
2. 'Abdu'l-Bahá, *'Abdu'l-Bahá in London*, pp. 95–96.

CHAPTER 5

1. The Universal House of Justice, *The Promise of World Peace: To the Peoples of the World,* p. 13.
2. Ibid., p. 13.
3. Bahá'u'lláh, *Gleanings,* nos. 131.2, 132.3.
4. Ibid., no. 132.3.
5. Ibid., no. 70.2.

CHAPTER 6

1. Adam's, T. H., Rev. *Portsmouth New Hampshire Weekly.*
2. Bahá'u'lláh, Hidden Words, Persian, no. 51.
3. Bahá'u'lláh, *Tablets of Bahá'u'lláh,* pp. 172–73.
4. Bahá'u'lláh, *Gleanings,* no. 106.1.

CHAPTER 7

1. Bahá'u'lláh, quoted in Shoghi Effendi, *The Advent of Divine Justice,* ¶40.
2. Rúmí, *The Essential Rúmí,* p. 168.

CHAPTER 8

1. Bahá'u'lláh, Hidden Words, Arabic, no. 51.
2. 'Abdu'l-Bahá, *Paris Talks,* no. 35.6.

CHAPTER 9

1. 'Abdu'l-Bahá, *Some Answered Questions,* p. 231.
2. Bahá'u'lláh, The Kitáb-i-Aqdas, Notes, no. 88.
3. 'Abdu'l-Bahá, *Selections from the Writings of 'Abdu'l-Bahá,* no. 88.2.
4. Ibid., no. 88.1.
5. Bahá'u'lláh, The Kitáb-i-Aqdas, Questions and Answers, no. 3.
6. Bahá'u'lláh, *Epistle to the Son of the Wolf,* p. 32.
7. Ibid., p. 32.

CHAPTER *10*

1. 'Abdu'l-Bahá, *Star of the West,* vol. 4, no. 18, p. 305.
2. 'Abdu'l-Bahá, *Promulgation of Universal Peace,* p. 52.
3. Bahá'u'lláh, *Gleanings,* no. 27.2.
4. Bahá'u'lláh, The Hidden Words, Arabic, no. 12.
5. Ibid., Arabic, no. 11.
6. 'Abdu'l-Bahá, *Promulgation of Universal Peace,* p. 471.

CHAPTER *11*

1. Teilhard de Chardin, http://www.wisdomquotes.com/003647.html.

CHAPTER *12*

1. Shoghi Effendi, *God Passes By,* p. xiv.
2. Nabíl, *The Dawn-Breakers,* p. 75.
3. Ibid., p. 93.
4. Bahá'u'lláh, *Gleanings,* no. 4.1–2.
5. Bahá'u'lláh, *The Proclamation of Bahá'u'lláh,* p. v.
6. Bahá'u'lláh, quoted in Shoghi Effendi, *God Passes By,* p. 222.
7. 'Alí-Akbar Furútan, *Stories of Bahá'u'lláh,* p. 109.

CHAPTER *14*

1. Bahá'u'lláh, *The Seven Valleys and The Four Valleys,* p. 34.
2. Bahá'u'lláh, *Gleanings,* no. 110.1.

CHAPTER *15*

1. Bahá'u'lláh, The Hidden Words, Persian, no. 49.
2. Bahá'u'lláh, *Gleanings,* nos. 112.1 and 117.1.

WORKS CITED

Works of Bahá'u'lláh

Epistle to the Son of the Wolf. Translated by Shoghi Effendi. 1st pocket-size ed. Wilmette, IL: Bahá'í Publishing Trust, 1988.

Gleanings from the Writings of Bahá'u'lláh. Translated by Shoghi Effendi. Wilmette, IL: Bahá'í Publishing, 2005.

The Hidden Words. Translated by Shoghi Effendi. Wilmette, IL: Bahá'í Publishing, 2002.

The Kitáb-i-Aqdas: The Most Holy Book. 1st pocket-sized ed. Wilmette, IL: Bahá'í Publishing Trust, 1993.

The Kitáb-i-Íqán: The Book of Certitude. Translated by Shoghi Effendi. Wilmette, IL: Bahá'í Publishing, 2003.

Prayers and Meditations. Translated by Shoghi Effendi. 1st pocket-size ed. Wilmette, IL: Bahá'í Publishing Trust, 1987.

The Proclamation of Bahá'u'lláh to the Kings and Leaders of the World. Haifa: Bahá'í World Center, 1972.

The Seven Valleys and The Four Valleys. Translated by Marzieh Gail in consultation with Ali-Kuli Khan. Wilmette, IL: Bahá'í Publishing Trust, 1991.

Tablets of Bahá'u'lláh revealed after the Kitáb-i-Aqdas. Compiled by the Research Department of the Universal House of Justice. Translated by Habib Taherzadeh et al. Wilmette, IL: 1988.

Works of 'Abdu'l-Bahá

'Abdu'l-Bahá in London: Addresses and Notes of Conversations. London: Bahá'í Publishing Trust, 1982.

Paris Talks: Addresses Given by 'Abdu'l-Bahá in Paris in 1911. Wilmette, IL: Bahá'í Publishing, 2006.

The Promulgation of Universal Peace: Talks Delivered by 'Abdu'l-Bahá during His Visit to the United States and Canada in 1912. Compiled by Howard MacNutt. New ed. Wilmette, IL: Bahá'í Publishing, 2007.

Selections from the Writings of 'Abdu'l-Bahá. Compiled by the Research Department of the Universal House of Justice. Translated by a Committee at the Bahá'í World Center and by Marzieh Gail. 1st pocket-sized ed. Wilmette, IL: Bahá'í Publishing Trust, 1996.

Some Answered Questions. Compiled and translated by Laura Clifford Barney. Wilmette, IL: Bahá'í Publishing Trust, 2008.

"The Three Realities." *Star of the West* 7, no. 13 (1916): 117–19, 124.

Works of Shoghi Effendi

The Advent of Divine Justice. New ed. Wilmette, IL: Bahá'í Publishing Trust, 2006.
God Passes By. Rev. ed. Wilmette, IL: Bahá'í Publishing Trust, 1974.

Works of the Universal House of Justice

Messages from the Universal House of Justice: 1963–1986, The Third Epoch of the Formative Age. Compiled by Geoffry Marks. Wilmette, IL: Bahá'í Publishing Trust, 1996.
The Promise of World Peace: To the Peoples of the World. Wilmette, IL: Bahá'í Publishing Trust, 1985.

Bahá'í Compilations

Bahá'í Prayers: A Selection of Prayers Revealed by Bahá'u'lláh, the Báb, and 'Abdu'l-Bahá. Wilmette, IL: Bahá'í Publishing Trust, 2008.

Other Works

Adams, T. H., Rev. Washington's Runaway Slave, and How Portsmouth Freed Her. *The Granite Freeman,* May 22, 1845. Reprinted in *Portsmouth New Hampshire Weekly,* June 2, 1877.
Furútan, 'Alí-Akbar. *Stories of Bahá'u'lláh.* Translated by Katayoon and Robert Crerar and others. Oxford: George Ronald, 1986.
Gibran, Khalil. *The Prophet.* New York: Alfred A. Knopf, 1973.
Nabíl-i-A'zam (Muḥammad-i-Zarandí). *The Dawn-Breakers: Nabíl's Narrative of the Early Days of the Bahá'í Revelation.* Translated and edited by Shoghi Effendi. Wilmette, IL: Bahá'í Publishing Trust, 1999.
Rúmí. *The Essential Rúmí.* Translated by Coleman Barks, San Francisco: HarperOne, 1997.
True, Corinne. From *Table Talks by Abdul-Baha.* "The Divine Wisdom in Fasting." *Star of the West* 4, no. 18 (1914): 305.

WHO IS PHYLLIS EDGERLY RING?

A freelance writer for more than twenty years, Phyllis Edgerly Ring has published in a wide variety of print and electronic media. She has contributed to such anthologies as *Chicken Soup for Every Mom's Soul*, and *Traveller's Tales*, and for eight years, her "Ringside" column was a monthly feature in the New Hampshire publications *The Portsmouth Herald*, *The Exeter News-letter*, and *The Hampton Union*. She has written for nationally circulated newspapers that include *Christian Science Monitor* and *American Profile*, and she has been a columnist for United Press International's Religionandspirituality.com Web site, exploring how the spiritual side of life reveals itself in our everyday experiences. Her articles and essays have appeared in dozens of magazines, including *Writer's Digest*, *Bay Area Parent*, *Ms.*, *Natural Awakenings*, *The World & I*, and *Yankee*. Her writing addresses a variety of topics including arts and culture, health and healing, parenting and family life, spirituality and inspiration, and travel. In 2002, she received a Media Excellence Award from the National Foundation for Women Legislators and previously received first-place awards from the New Hampshire Press Association and the Brass Ring Writing-the-Web Competition. She was formerly the features editor for a New Hampshire newspaper group, has served as program coordinator at Green Acre Bahá'í School in Eliot, Maine, and has taught English and virtues to kindergartners in Shanghai, China.

She is a member of the International Women's Writing Guild and has served as a writing instructor for the Long Ridge Writer's Group since 2001. A guest speaker and workshop facilitator for many organizations and conferences, she addresses the writer's craft, parenting and family life, issues of race and gender equality, child development and spirituality, virtues- and character-education, and spiritual growth and transformation.

PUBLICATION CREDITS

"Baked with Loving Hands" was previously published in March 2005 in *Chicken Soup for Every Mom's Soul*.

"Cultivating a Culture of Encouragement" was previously published in the March 2004 issue of *Sasee*.

"Each Day a New Beginning" was previously published under the title "Spring Promises the Blessings of Renewal" in the April 2006 issue of *Sasee*.

"Every True Gift Has Eternity in It" was previously published under the title "Small Packages" in the July 2004 issue of *Mamm*.

"The Gift of a Winter's Grace," was previously published in the April 2006 issue of *The Portsmouth Herald*.

"Hope Blossoms with Prayer" was previously published under the title "Hope Blossoms" in the March 2003 issue of *Mamm*.

"How to Avoid a Big Stink" was previously published in the July 11, 2005, issue of *Christian Science Monitor*.

"The Legacy of a Happy Heart" was previously published under the title "What Marian Shared" in the July 1984 issue of *Unity*.

"A Life with Room for Dying" was previously published in the November 2005 issue of *The Portsmouth Herald*.

"Little Angel, Big Prayer" was previously published in September 2007 in *A Chicken Soup for the Soul Christmas*.

"My Father's New Garden" was previously published in the July 2007 issue of *The Portsmouth Herald*.

"Not Nearly Enough" was previously published under the title "A Burger and a Win over Prejudice" in the February 13, 2006, issue of *Christian Science Monitor.*

"The Remedy Resides in Us" was previously published in the September 11, 2006, issue of *Christian Science Monitor.*

"Small Change" was previously published in *Living.*

"Some Pennies Just Might Be from Heaven" was previously published in *Miracles of Healing* (Carmel, NY: Guidepost Books, 2006).

Bahá'í
PUBLISHING
and the Bahá'í Faith

Bahá'í Publishing produces books based on the teachings of the Bahá'í Faith. Founded over 160 years ago, the Bahá'í Faith has spread to some 235 nations and territories and is now accepted by more than five million people. The word "Bahá'í" means "follower of Bahá'u'lláh." Bahá'u'lláh, the founder of the Bahá'í Faith, asserted that He is the Messenger of God for all of humanity in this day. The cornerstone of His teachings is the establishment of the spiritual unity of humankind, which will be achieved by personal transformation and the application of clearly identified spiritual principles. Bahá'ís also believe that there is but one religion and that all the Messengers of God—among them Abraham, Zoroaster, Moses, Krishna, Buddha, Jesus, and Muḥammad—have progressively revealed its nature. Together, the world's great religions are expressions of a single, unfolding divine plan. Human beings, not God's Messengers, are the source of religious divisions, prejudices, and hatreds.

The Bahá'í Faith is not a sect or denomination of another religion, nor is it a cult or a social movement. Rather, it is a globally recognized independent world religion founded on new books of scripture revealed by Bahá'u'lláh.

Bahá'í Publishing is an imprint of the National Spiritual Assembly of the Bahá'ís of the United States.

For more information about the Bahá'í Faith,
or to contact Bahá'ís near you, visit
http://www.bahai.us/
or call
1-800-22-unite

Other Books Available from Bahá'í Publishing

Creative Dimensions of Suffering
A-M. GHADIRIAN, M.D.
$15.00 U.S. / $17.00 CAN
Trade Paper
ISBN 978-1-931847-60-5

A noted professor and psychiatrist explores the link between suffering, creativity, and spirituality

Creative Dimensions of Suffering draws upon the author's personal knowledge and experience as a psychiatrist, as well as extensive research through literature on suffering, to explore the enigmatic and intriguing connection between creativity and suffering. He examines the lives of many artists, writers, poets, and scientists, as well as ordinary individuals, who have risen above their own suffering and left behind a legacy of unique and amazing experiences. Among these are well-known figures such as van Gogh, Tchaikovsky, Beethoven, Helen Keller, and Christopher Reeve. Examining their lives for insight into how they dealt with their adversity through creativity, he also explores how various conditions such as alcoholism, depression, bipolar disorder, and dementia can influence a person's creative impulse and how the interplay of creativity and spirituality can help a person deal with trauma and hardship.

Drawing on principles found in the teachings of the Bahá'í Faith, Dr. Ghadirian considers the meaning of suffering, its place in human society, and how it can lead to a closer, happier relationship with God, as well as a better relationship with oneself and with others. Indeed, many of those who have suffered the most in life have found new meaning through adversity and have emerged victorious. Their encounters with adversity and their victory over it suggest the presence of another force beyond understanding that reinforces the individual during periods of intense suffering.

High Desert

A Journey of Survival and Hope
KIM DOUGLAS
$20.00 U.S. / $22.00 CAN
Trade Paper
ISBN 978-1-931847-59-9

A deeply moving memoir with a holistic approach to overcoming the effects of growing up in a severely abusive home

High Desert is a courageous, gripping, and deeply personal autobiographical account about growing up in an abusive home and finding a path to recovery by learning to rely on faith and spiritual beliefs to heal and grow in ways that go beyond traditional twelve-step programs and other approaches. In this eye-opening account, Kim Douglas reveals a wide range of issues and behaviors that will be familiar to many who have come from similar circumstances: eating disorders, obsessive or compulsive behaviors, and troubled relationships with friends and family members. Most important is the author's insight and experience in finding effective ways of coping with life's challenges, learning to trust others in a close relationship, parenting without repeating the cycle of abuse, healing the relationship with the abuser, and forgiving those who don't help in a time of crisis.

Illumine My Family

Prayers and Meditations from the Bahá'í Faith
BAHÁ'U'LLÁH, THE BÁB, AND 'ABDU'L-BAHÁ
Compiled by Bahá'í Publishing
$12.00 U.S. / $13.50 CAN
Trade Paper
ISBN 978-1-931847-62-9

A heartwarming collection of prayers for people of all faiths to meet the challenges of everyday life

Illumine My Family is a collection of prayers and meditative passages from the writings of the Bahá'í Faith that will help any family wishing to incorporate spirituality into their daily lives. The passages included offer guidance and prayers on subjects relevant to any family regardless of their background or current circumstances. Subjects covered include marriage, parents, motherhood, children, love, healing, the loss of a loved one, and more. The book has been put together with the hope that it will assist families to grow together and to foster strong relationships with each other and with God.

The Universe Within Us
A Guide to the Purpose of Life
JANE E. HARPER
$15.00 U.S. / $17.00 CAN
Trade Paper
ISBN 978-1-931847-58-2

A provocative look at the purpose of life through a mixture of religion, science, and personal experience

Author Jane E. Harper offers insight into a new way to look at life. *The Universe Within Us* is a mixture of science, religion, and personal experience that offers a new understanding of our place and purpose in the universe— an understanding that leads to the conclusion that every human being possesses a spiritual nature. Harper argues that, traditionally, answers to questions about the purpose of life have long been the domain of priests and clergy, and, more recently, scientists—and often the answers have been less than satisfying. The religious answers often leave the intellect out and defy what the rational mind can accept, while the scientific answers satisfy the intellect at the expense of the heart and soul. Drawing on resources available from the sciences, from the world's sacred scriptures, and from personal observations and experiences, she offers a unique map of the universe and an explanation of life's purpose that is truly satisfying.

To view our complete catalog,
Please visit http://books.bahai.us